P9-CBG-766

SOPHISTICATION

SOPHISTICATION

Rhetoric & the Rise of Self-Consciousness

Mark Backman

INDIANA-
PURDUE
LIBRARY
WITHDRAWN]
FORT WAYNE

PN
175
.B14
1991

OX BOW PRESS
WOODBRIDGE, CONNECTICUT

Copyright © 1991 by Mark Backman
All rights reserved.

Publisher
Ox Bow Press
P.O. Box 4045
Woodbridge, CT 06525
Producer
Zachary Morowitz
Printer
Thomson-Shore, Inc.
Dexter, Michigan

Library of Congress Cataloging-in-Publication Data
Backman, Mark
    Sophistication: rhetoric and the rise of self-consciousness.
    Includes bibliographical references.
    ISBN 0-918024-91-9 (alk. paper)
    1. Rhetoric. I. Title
PN175.B14   1991
808--dc20   91-31004

The paper used in this book meets the guidelines for permanence
and durability of the Committee on Production Guidelines for
Book Longevity of the Council on Library Resources.

PRINTED IN THE UNITED STATES OF AMERICA

To Louis McNew
philosopher, teacher, friend

Acknowledgments

A BOOK LIKE THIS does not spring completely formed from a single mind. It evolves out of innumerable conversations and confrontations. It is less an original invention than it is the residue of intellectual interaction over time. The arrangement of the ideas into this form, however, is the primary contribution I can claim to the history of ideas. And that formation of thought was greatly assisted by several people. First, there are the numerous friends whose support for this project always seemed to be expressed at those moments when I was flagging in the effort and needed to be told that it was worthwhile. Then there are the several employers and business partners who made it possible for me to write *and* make a living, an oxymoronic concept if ever there was one. Finally, there are those who in one way or another had a direct hand in helping me with the process of writing and thinking. Special thanks are their due. My sister, Lynda Cox, who linked my often theoretical notions to the realities of life and labor. Professor John Ehrstine of Washington State University, whose keen eye and discerning ear were applied to my prose, my ideas and my intentions throughout this project. The late Professor Janette Richardson of the University of California at Berkeley, who found merit in a young graduate student with interests and inclinations that did not conform strictly to the academic regimen of which she was the premier exemplar. Zachary Morowitz, whose common sense, ability, and intelligence not only make him the best editor but also the best of friends as well. And finally, Louis McNew, to whom this book is dedicated and without whom it would not have been written. He helped me discover my mind and had the wisdom to let me apply it as best I could.

Preface

I CAME TO THE IDEAS in this book by an indirect path. It began in a solitary childhood where observation and imagination united to produce a mind that knew at an early age that things are rarely as they seem to be. It was a fundamental and profound discovery that led naturally to the perception of the world as a place often characterized by ambiguity, misdirection and even subterfuge.

Those observations were strengthened by an education that focused on the power of language to shape many different transient realities. These realities are the products not only of literature, art and other kinds of fictive representation. They are also an integral part of everyday life in a world ordered by self-interest, self-confidence and self-deception. Consequently, my education took place not only in the classroom, as both a student and a teacher, but also in the world at large. I began applying these ideas to all sorts of tasks on behalf of clients in business and politics, from writing speeches to reorganizing the management of work. The early lessons of my life were thus transformed into universal principles about the power of words and images to shape the very circumstances of expression.

The ideas in this book are at once personal and communal. They arose from the encounter with my own opinions and attitudes, fears and desires, powers and weaknesses, successes and failures, courage and cowardice as well as those of other people. They are neither novel nor wholly of my own invention. They flow to me, and through me, from the same archaic sources which nourish every self-conscious mind. I leave them here with my own imprint affixed firmly to them, for this book reveals on every page a particular handling of received opinion and common knowledge.

This book thus embodies in both form and content the essential paradox which it also attempts to reveal: that individual being can neither be isolated from nor enslaved by the historical, political, educational, ethical and aesthetic circumstances of social character. The mind that would come to terms with itself must also come to terms with the complexities of its times. And though it may have the power to invent its own past and to create its own present, the self-conscious mind remains a frail thing indeed when it confronts its own future.

Seattle, Washington
September, 1991

Contents

SOPHISTICATION

CHAPTER ONE

The Roots of
Our Sophistication

To know the world, one must construct it.
—Cesare Pavese

Be careful how you interpret the world; it is like that.
—Erich Heller

W E LIVE IN AN AGE POWERED by assumptions about language and reality that took root in Greece during the fifth century B.C., when the relationship between individuals and communities underwent a sea change. It was during this time that civilization as we know it emerged from the thrall of mythic history. Human beings began to take hold of their lives and their destinies as conscious agents of change. They recognized the power of the mind to alter reality through words and images. And they grasped for the first time the notion that individual being is determined in the context of social character, that we come to know ourselves through the motivated interaction with other people.

These innovations are the roots of self-consciousness. Without a sense of destiny, empowerment and community, humankind would have remained wrapped in the fog of superstition and credulity. The Greeks, however, set us on another path. It leads away from the security and confinement of the self-contained, self-explained existence. Instead, it courses through a landscape marked by uncertainty and doubt and confusion.

Despite its obvious virtues, the Greek gift of self-consciousness has proven to be a mixed blessing for it entails an essential paradox. What is gained in knowledge and power is tempered by the realization of inadequacy and impotence.

This much was known at the very beginning, when the instigators of these innovations first moved among the citizens of Athens promising to help them find the good life in a world undergoing rapid, irreversible change. They were called *sophists* and their message was simple and direct: "You have the power to change your life. Every man is equal, none enjoys natural advantages. Man himself is the measure of all things. We do not even know if the gods exist. The question is irrelevant." These assertions undermined the traditional moral foundations of community and upended static social arrangements that had bound citizens together longer than anyone could remember. Those of wealth and power found them subversive and danger-ous. But the idea that an individual could seize opportunity and control fate, rather than be victimized by the decisions of others, was potent elixir for a people who were also claiming for the first time in Western Culture to be sovereign among themselves.

The term "sophist" derives from the Greek *sophos* and *sophia*, "wise" and "wisdom," as does a related word, "philosopher," a lover of wisdom. In archaic times, *sophia* was the exclusive trait of poets and prophets who possessed special insight into things unrealized by mere mortals. *Sophia* was magical in both its ori-gins and effects for it dealt with a way of seeing beyond the limits of physical sense. During the fifth century B.C., however, the term "sophist" attached to a special class of itinerant educators who also claimed to possess insight into the workings of human nature. They were self-proclaimed citizens of the world, self-conscious innovators and accomplished self-promoters. They were rootless and iconoclastic in a culture that valued homeland and tradition. Consequently, the sophists acquired a reputation for a kind of intellectual disorderly conduct. They seemed to overthrow many of the ideas that were at the center of commu-nal life. They preached a reliance on individual initiative, intel-lect and the mastery of public presentation, all of which were fast becoming the essential ingredients of success in the burgeoning Greek democracies. Any person could gain power over other minds if only they would submit to an education that produced a sophisticated appreciation of language and power.

"Sophist" is also at the heart of our concept of sophistication, the much sought after quality that distinguishes one person or idea or invention from all others. It values the worldly-wise, the experienced, the tested and the refined. In a culture where the disintegration of long-established rules of thought, expression and action imperils both sense and sensibility, sophistication becomes the yardstick against which to measure success in life. It is the speed of light in a universe based on the relativity of human values and beliefs. In ancient Athens, the sophists came to stand for all that was new and exciting. They reflected in their clothes and adornments the new emphasis on material wealth. They reflected in their habit of mind the new wisdom of the public meeting place, where every opinion could be asserted freely but only the eloquent and articulate was heard. They embodied, that is, the emerging sophistication of culture.

To sophisticate something, however, also means to deprive it of its simplicity and genuineness. Sophistication is an artificial construction, a product of social intercourse. It is the antithesis of naturalism and the opposite of naivete, for sophistication is a mindful state. There are no accidental sophisticates, in art or life. Most important of all, sophistication plays on emotion and it relies on the force of an articulate personality although, at times, it is disguised as reasonableness, modesty and even humility. Pursued relentlessly, sophistication leads to disillusionment and cynicism, for worldly wisdom always entails abandoning illusions and confronting unadorned realities.

Thus by instruction as well as by example the sophists introduced the Western mind to the paradoxes of sophistication. At one level, it is a state of being marked not only by cultural refinement, intellectual currency, and social domination but, more important, by self-consciousness. At another level, sophistication is a process of becoming something else, of shedding one set of attitudes and beliefs and of assuming another. At any moment in time, the standards of sophistication can be fixed against the shifting background of social development. Thus, manners and attitudes considered sophisticated fifty years ago appear quaint and precious to us today. Sophistication as a state of being is always at war with sophistication as a process of becoming. Sophistic education aims to teach a mode of presentation and performance that *in the moment of its execution* embodies the highest expression of the sophisticated mind. It is an ambitious and unsettling pedagogy.

Sophistication is based on practical innovation, the foundation of creativity in all realms of action. In any age, ancient or modern, the sophisticate has been a pragmatic sort, more a doer than a thinker. The world and its constraints are his reality. Intellectual acuity, expressed at one extreme as mere cleverness and at another as eccentric genius, is the key to prosperity in a fickle, changing universe. The Greek sophists exercised a passion for exploring the fundamental questions of life in community. What are the duties a citizen owes his city? Is it possible to teach leadership? What determines righteous action—individual conscience, the dictates of the state, or religious piety? Does might make right? Can virtue be taught? Are words more real than ideas? Do ideas exist if they are unspoken? Is knowledge of concrete things or abstract ideas? Is it possible to know anything at all? Is there one Truth or many? How do we distinguish the true from the apparently true? Questions like these are not merely of theoretical interest when they are addressed in the crucible of self-governance. They possess a profoundly practical dimension.

Sophistication is shaped by the principles and techniques of persuasive communication. Although they belonged to no formal school of thought, the ancient sophists made their living by teaching what we would recognize as courses in self-improvement. Their program was embodied in an art of persuasion that emphasized the potency of the plausible claim asserted at the opportune moment. It was primarily concerned with the creation and presentation of compelling arguments within the context of group decision-making. These were promulgated in figurative language that, according to the theory of the time, exerted a kind of power over the soul. Persuasion through language could make things appear to be quite different from what had originally been thought to be the case. The sophists promised to empower anyone who could pay their fees to succeed in the law courts, the marketplace, the world at large—in any circumstance, that is, where opinion and belief are the basis of judgment and suasive language is the determinant of action.

Sophistication grounds reality in the relativity of truth. The Greek sophists were the first minds in Western history to realize that thinking, speaking and doing are distinct realms of creativity related in the most complex, reflexive fashion. Thought, expression and action shape, and are shaped by, the circumstances within which they occur. This characteristic of sophistic thought manifests itself in the radical belief that there is no truth other than that which can be agreed upon. Suasive expression is not only an instrument for the discussion of facts but, more important, it is a cause of their invention as well. The sophists distinguished between appearance and reality in a manner that even today animates and orders the practice of politics, public relations and public performance in all the sciences and arts.

Because the Greek sophists promoted sophistication in the face of values they considered provincial, naive and irrelevant, they play a paradoxical role in the march to self-consciousness. On one hand, they initiated what is now called the Greek Enlightenment, a flowering of knowledge that spread throughout the ancient world and altered forever the way human beings thought about their communities, their fellow citizens and their selves. On the other hand, their thinking led to the collapse of beliefs and ideas that had stabilized culture for centuries. Their challenge to tradition fostered immediate opposition not only among the vested political and religious interests of the day but also from other speculative thinkers.

Their earliest opponent, Socrates, clearly opposed the sophistic tendency to put man at the center of things and to make virtue a mere residue of power. His disciple Plato can be credited with setting the pejorative judgment that has dogged the sophists to this day. For him, the sophist is an unscrupulous dilettante, someone who would argue both sides of a question with equal skill and commitment and with an utter lack of regard to the facts or the consequences of the argument. That judgment still guides our own sense of the term, for sophist and sophistry are now exclusively associated with fallacious logic, specious reasoning and unprincipled argument. Still, sophistic learning spurred freedom of thought and speech, technical proficiency and intellectual creativity, all virtues readily admired by the Greeks and by us. For these reasons, Plato's student Aristotle attempts to accommodate the sophistic impulse within a coherent system of thought, expression and action. He tries to tame the beast of sophistry that Plato banishes from his own well-ordered republic.

Plato's reaction to the sophists and Aristotle's accommodation of their assumptions are attempts to reconstitute the very idea of sophistication. Neither Plato nor Aristotle advocates a return to the old ways, to naivete and credulity. Both seek an alternative to grounding self-consciousness in the free flowing circumstances of changeable opinions and expedient beliefs. However we judge their efforts, Plato and Aristotle are the headwaters for two of the three streams of philosophical thought in Western Culture. The sophists animate the third, more subtle yet equally important flow in the history of ideas.

Each of these streams enters our time under many guises and by many names. The original debate between Plato, Aristotle and the sophists has become sophisticated in its own right. The intervening centuries have deposited an overlay of terms and concepts in successive sedimentary layers that appear distinct and novel yet which upon closer inspection can be seen to blend one into the other. In their complicated totality they mask the relative simplicity that orders the history of ideas in the West. The differences between Plato, Aristotle and the sophists have been treated for the most part as historical and circumstantial, tied as they are to the astonishing 150 years that separate the birth of Socrates in 469 B.C. from the death of Aristotle in 322 B.C. But a more lively and relevant analysis can be made, one that tells us something about ourselves as well as about the ancient Greeks. It focuses on how each of the three streams of thought conceives of history, politics, education, ethics and aesthetics as *operational* concepts in everyday life. It illuminates the nature of sophistication as a concept of social organization and of personal identity. Most important, such analysis reveals a central principle agreed upon by Plato, Aristotle and the sophists: language is essential to the sophistication of culture as well as to the discovery of self-consciousness.

As the key to the observation, articulation and creation of reality, language not only expresses what we know, it is also knowledge in physical form. It is a cause of effects. It brings into being what would never be brought into being without it. It operates. What we now mean by language has evolved to reflect the manifold complexity of modern forms of expression. As a descriptive term, language no longer delineates the province of words, though these are still the essential vehicles of communication. Rather, it now encompasses all symbolization—in words or numbers or pictures or images—which operates as a body of knowledge, the embodiment of culture and the cause of effects. Nor is language simply a national or ethnic or cultural invention. It is also a product of technological sophistication, of the demands for precision and exclusivity that grow out of the manipulation of discrete sciences for predictable, productive ends. Nor is language a natural phenomenon. It is an artificial construction, represented as much by the digitalized code of the electronic computer as by the organized noise of human talk. Language is at once affective and effective, for it not only embodies our knowledge, emotions and desires; it also has the power to stir our minds and souls.

The intellectual innovation that transformed the ancient world, and has transformed our own as well, turns on a fundamentally important fact. There is a real difference between what people say, what they mean and what they do. We learn at an early age to exploit the lack of trustworthy connections between words, thoughts and actions. *Pretending* and *imitating* are the most essential kinds of child's play. Adults employ these skills with greater subtlety and precision borne of self-conscious intent. Pretense and imitation are powerful capacities of the mature mind. They allow us to stand beside ourselves, to seem to be something or someone else. They are the basic instruments of all great actors, the essential components of irony and the basis of a well-developed sense of humor. They are stimulated by the demands and expectations of others. We pretend and imitate with an audience in mind. The necessity of living with other people prevents us from dwelling too long on the little subversions of meaning and confidence, imagined or real, that mark our lives. It is too difficult and too painful to lead a completely honest life, a child's life. A person's sophistication is signalled by the ability to invent shortcuts through the thicket of conflicting words and actions. We do so in order to protect ourselves from human guile, our own and that of other people, as well as to promote our interests in the face of beguiling competition. In every case, the press of mundane matters leads away from the center of things, the core of private, solitary being that asserts itself in the quiet but momentous occasions of life.

Somewhere along the line, each of us realizes that words and thoughts and deeds are often out of whack, and not just because other people are malevolent or devious. A much more complicated explanation of human behavior is required, one that goes beyond the apparently vivid truths and falsities attendant to a psychology of absolute integrity. For people often use language without guile and not always with clear intentions. They can be alternately unknowing or aware, bold or fearful, rash or timid, exuberant or depressed, trusting or suspicious, skeptical or confident, arrogant or humble, precise or ambiguous. As a consequence, human expression is at once troubled and troubling; our smug claims to master it are but an act of bravado, like whistling as we pass the graveyard.

In self-defense as much as in self-promotion, each of us exercises to some degree the power to interpret another person's statements and deeds. We impute intentions and motives, speculate about causes and effects, and concoct analyses and explanations that justify to ourselves—and to anyone who will listen—that matters stand as we see them. When our opinion is borne out by tangible results in the external world, little thought is given to the validity of our assumptions or the accuracy of our analysis. Rightness, after all, ought to be self-evident. It is only when we fail that we begin to look for reasons and construct explanations.

These characteristics of communication are the basis for a

sophisticated appreciation of the causes and effects of language that in antiquity acquired a name and a reputation that are well known in our own day. At the heart of sophisticated culture resides a paradoxical art of such power and vitality that it has become synonymous with persuasion in all its aspects: manipulation, reasoning, discourse, negotiation, trickery and fraud. It has evolved from a set of effective techniques used by orators of the fifth century B.C. into a highly refined art of analysis and articulation. What the Greeks first called *rhetoric* encompasses the technical, psychological and formal aspects of communication. Their conception of this sophisticated art is only hinted at by our present understanding of the word. We use the term rhetoric antithetically, to contrast abstract words from concrete things, style from substance. If a politician speaks in vague generalities, using emotional or colorful language, we say his speech is "mere rhetoric," meaning that it somehow lacks substance. Or we talk about the rhetoric of advertising or law or public relations or any number of other fields, as if the language of these arts is somehow distinct from the arts themselves. Or we distinguish between what a person says, his rhetoric, from what he means, his intention, or from what he does, his deed. As a descriptive term rhetoric has come to stand for empty style, clever speaking and fancy words.

Rhetoric, however, is much more than glib assertions and fast talk. Behind its manifold appearance as an art or a method or a form of persuasion, rhetoric is essentially an attitude about public expression and the nature of the world. It resides at the crux of the relationship between language and reality. The disposition to be rhetorical has always been controversial because it involves a kind of personal power, the capacity to influence the private thoughts of others through the public use of language. The modern conception of rhetoric reflects the vestiges of its almost mystical ancestry. In ancient Greece a great debate arose over the effects of words on the souls of men. This was no small matter for the Greeks who, by the fifth century B.C., were coming to realize that the motives of human action lay closer at hand than the mythic explanations seemed to indicate. The concept of individual responsibility was gaining ground against the traditional theology of divine interference and inspiration. The thesis that was put forth by the sophists was a radical one. Mortal minds, not the gods, determine the course of human events. The rise of rhetoric thus parallels the rise of self-consciousness in Western history. It is essentially a social and political phenomenon that involves the dawning awareness of the connection between the individual and his community. And these events further stirred the social, political and cultural ferment that marks the fifth century B.C. as a time of change very similar to our own. As the leading innovators of the day, the sophists were regarded with great ambivalence, either as harbingers of a new regime of thought and action or as destroyers of the old world. That paradoxical reputation and the odium it bears for rhetoric carries over to our time.

The rise of rhetoric entails persistent, fundamental questions about the relationship between thought, expression and action. The paradoxes that materialize when we try to answer these questions ripple through the structures, institutions and organizations we construct to express and enforce the communal will. Whether we like it or not, the theoretical and often abstract notions about the operations of the mind express themselves everyday in the way we make a living, elect our leaders, educate our young, deal with each other in work or in play and judge the products of human inventiveness. The elementary discovery of the Greeks, that the distinction between thought and action is ultimately an artificial one, also underwrites our own immersion in sophistic culture. The sophists' confidence in human potentiality exposes for us, as it did for the ancients, the three basic questions of epistemology: What do we know? How do we know that we know? How do we tell others what we know?

These questions have always accompanied the complex search for the basis of reality. "Knowing" has been the province of philosophers, psychologists and more recently the cyberneticists. Each has probed related areas such as cognition and perception. Each has developed analogies and metaphors to portray the mind's operations in terms at once familiar and mystical. As lovers of wisdom, philosophers regard knowledge as a state of perfected being, a desired condition that can be reached through instincts sharpened by practice and purification. As doctors of the soul, psychologists regard awareness as the residue of biological or physical or mental processes that are affected by, and interact with, natural stimulations outside the mind. As makers of artificial brains, cyberneticists conceive of consciousness as a primary constituent of synergistic electrical or mechanical or chemical interactions the total effect of which is greater than the sum of each as an independent force. In one way or another, all have developed schemes to describe the interaction between the senses and the mind. They have founded schools of thought supporting one or another conception of what it is to know. And they have speculated on the future development of human awareness, both in its own potency and as it is aided by the tools of modern technology. Whatever his school or sect, the epistemologist has held center stage in the history of ideas since the Greeks. That is because questions about the foundation and transmission of knowledge are crucial to any system that seeks to secure its past, preserve order, educate its members and control the future.

The sophist has always represented a dangerous tendency in the history of ideas. Because he holds no allegiance to specific theories or doctrines of knowledge, he is likely to be accused of intellectual dabbling and a lack of seriousness. But the sophist also develops a characteristic epistemology grounded in the circumstantial requirements of rhetoric, as a method of argument, an art of persuasion and a form of communication. He seeks the fundamental principles of power that put an individual in control of others.

The central role rhetoric plays in modern life flows from the pragmatic innovations of Tisias and Corax, two Greeks who lived in Sicily at the outset of the fifth century B.C. Their names are associated with the first known treatise on a rhetorical subject, the *Art of Words*, written around 460 B.C. Theirs is not an accidental invention, like the discovery of some natural element or chemical reaction. For a Greek living through the rise of democracy, the highest virtue was to be a good speaker as well as a man of action, to be a force in the community. The conjunction of expression and deed is one concrete manifestation of the complex epistemology of rhetoric that can be traced to Tisias and Corax. They are the first to treat the appeal to probability as a legitimate specie of legal reasoning. Lawyers ever since have taken advantage of its power.

Aristotle's discussion of rhetorical probability, in the next century, puts the matter plainly. A man accused of assault can either produce facts demonstrating convincingly that he did not commit the action, such as an alibi or an eyewitness account of his presence elsewhere, or make an argument from probability. If his alleged victim is larger and stronger, he may reason that it is unlikely for someone of his own size to attack such an imposing opponent. If, however, he is the stronger of the two he may maintain that only a fool would attack someone who is clearly inferior in strength. That only invites suspicion of the crime. The argument from probability reflects a key aspect of rhetoric: it is not the facts that matter so much as what can be said about them. Rhetoric, after all, is an art not only of speech and argument but also of appearance and belief. Invention is its engine and persuasion its goal.

The birth of rhetoric at the hands of Tisias and Corax coincides with the expulsion of the Syracusan tyrants and the establishment of democracy in the city and its environs. It was a time of great confusion and turmoil similar in many respects to contemporary developments in Eastern Europe where popular uprisings not only overthrow unpopular governments but, in the process, upend established ways of conducting the public's business. In fifth century Sicily, practical problems needed to be solved, not epistemological ones. Tisias and Corax sought a peaceful way of determining land ownership and tenancy rights, of deciding who could stay and who must be exiled in punishment for their collaboration with the old regime, and of settling a whole list of political and social grievances that previously had been resolved arbitrarily and often by force. The *Art of Words* is a practical handbook that promised to teach its reader how to make presentations before the assembly or in the law courts. Tisias and Corax do not regard rhetoric as we do, as some form of deception or fraud. The art they develop brings often violent oppositions together in order to solve problems that, left unaddressed, could tear the community apart. It substitutes speech, albeit speech which could take liberties with the truth, for force of arms. No wonder its popularity increased throughout the Greek world with the rise of democratic government, the rule of the many over the one, or the several. Rhetoric provides the basis for discussions of policy and the adjudication of disputes that until the fifth century were framed and settled quite differently, even capriciously, in the hands of absolute rulers or small groups of wealthy or powerful people, the oligarchs.

As intellectual concepts and as objective realities, the new art of rhetoric, the idea of individual freedom, and the novel emphasis on personal empowerment evolved hand-in-hand. Two "schools" of rhetoric emerged in Greece during the fifth century B.C. They both embody characteristic conceptions of knowledge and reality that distinguish the sophist's epistemology from all others. The first descends directly from Corax and Tisias and is concerned mainly with the art of persuasive presentation. Its ancient champion was Gorgias of Leontini (*c*. 485–380 B.C.), a student of the Sicilian duo. Modern scholars sometimes call this line of descent the Sicilian school since it was centered in Sicily and the adjacent Italian mainland. The second school is much more broadly gauged. It too focuses on persuasion and the appropriate use of language. But it quickly grew to encompass the education of the citizen in its widest sense, a concern of ours as well as of the ancient Greeks. Its most famous promoter was Protagoras (*c*. 490–421 B.C.), the originator of the famous aphorism "Man is the measure of all things." This branch of rhetoric is sometimes referred to as the Athenian school although, like most sophists, its members roamed widely throughout the Greek world.

Gorgias travelled widely, visiting Athens on an embassy from Leontini in 427 B.C. His long life encompasses the rise and fall of the Athenian empire. His specialty was persuasive speaking and he developed his art within the context of city-state politics. In Greece the successful man was one who could dominate the world of politics, and public speaking was clearly a necessary skill. Rhetoric, as an art of persuasion, held center court in the city-states of the emerging Greek democracies. In one of his works, Gorgias calls speech and persuasion the two irresistible forces of the universe. That universe, in turn, is controlled by some fundamental principles of reality and knowledge. Truth is local, specific to an individual and his circumstances. It is therefore also temporary since change is the one sure constant of the sophistic universe. A person ages, events pass, opinions shift, oppositions dissolve, life moves on, people forget. In such a world there is only belief and supposition rather than substantial knowledge about things.

"Persuasion allied to words can mold men's minds," according to Gorgias. Even the theories of science are at heart verbal representations, mere assertions in suasive language of underlying prejudices and presumptions. Each scientist thinks that his system contains the secret reality of the universe but he is actually only asserting his own opinion against others. He creates the illusion of certainty by petitioning the imagination through fanciful, appealing metaphors and figurative speech. Moreover, the debates and discussions of everyday life, especially in the courts or before the assembly, show that a single speech can turn a crowd from one opinion to another just because it is delightfully written, clever or novel, not because it is based on the truth. The waywardness of public opinion, then, is a fact beyond dispute and its existence alone proves that there is no such thing as the truth. Finally, the philosophers themselves provide proof of the power of persuasion, the fickleness of the mind and the absence of unchanging truths when they purport to reveal an immutable basis for reality. Their opinions are at once convincing and contradictory, no one exhibiting the universal proof he needs and all of them together showing by their very discord and division the overpowering domination of opinions and beliefs over truth. The Gorgian view of a reality based ultimately in persuasion and language, however, also makes him relevant to our own day. Among other things he introduced in his treatise *On the Right Moment in Time* the notion that rhetoric is an art of opportunity and timeliness. Persuasion occurs only when the elements of speech, the mood of the audience and the circumstances of expression are brought into alignment by the persuader.

The concept of probability that Corax and Tisias introduce into legal argument and the sense of opportunity that Gorgias places at the center of rhetoric are two of three cornerstones of ancient sophistic thought. The third is most clearly enunciated by Protagoras, who believed that all perceptions and judgments are relative to the perceiver. His "man is the measure" succinctly expresses the underlying confidence in human ingenuity that inspires all the sophists. *Every* human being is the measure of *all* things. Neither the high-born aristocrat nor the religious initiate possess any greater intellectual capacity than the common man. Protagoras values above all else the creative capacity of the human mind.

If there is no truth, as Gorgias declares, and if every man makes the truth for himself, "yours for you, mine for me" in his words, then the universe is devoid of absolute standards and humans are left to fend for themselves. In such a condition the only reality is that which can be agreed upon. This phenomenon of the human condition accounts for the varying traditions, laws and customs that can be detected in different communities, "even among the barbarians." Paradoxically, it is also binds all humans together despite obvious social or cultural differences. Every person possesses the faculty for invention. According to Protagoras, this permits us to create the different arts that make civilization a specifically human achievement. For the sophisticate of our time, such thinking is merely common sense. We are the heirs, not the originators, of the egocentric view of nature. But in Athens this pervasive relativity was radical and alarming, especially when it touched on politics and religion.

The key concepts passed on to us by Corax and Tisias, Gorgias and Protagoras—probability, opportunity and relativity—underwrite a radical epistemology. Knowledge is not based on systematic first principles. Rather, it inheres in the effects it has on the circumstances of expression. It is the residue of the mind at work in a setting, not an abstraction of mental processes or a collection of facts drawn from experience. The proof is in the pudding for a sophist. Results take priority over premises. Knowledge is functional order imposed for some specific end and rhetoric is the primary instrument for its institution.

Rhetoric takes its starting point in crisis, uncertainty, and opinion and is successful if it leads to a semblance of order. Consequently, although it lacks the metaphysical features found in philosophy and psychology and cybernetics, rhetoric is an epistemological art of the highest degree. It apprehends, defines, shapes, preserves, embodies and transmits the most fundamental kind of knowledge, that of the consequences of action exercised to some end. It is not concerned with collecting facts about the natural world but with assembling and disposing opinions that animate the social world. Rhetoric deals with the artificial structures of reality that in their compound complexities constitute what we call culture. We do it an injustice to define it simply as communication, as if a listing of items to be bought at the store reflects the power of the rhetorical epistemology. Ours is not a world of lists and facts. It is a paradoxical place composed of biases and prejudices, ambiguities and confusions, half-truths and outright lies, muddled intentions and prescient thoughts, wishes and fears. Self-confidence, emboldened and implemented by a positivistic art of rhetoric, cuts through the uncertainty, indecision and suspicion of daily life and offers us a program. Man is the measure of all things. To say is to do. And to do is to be.

Rhetoric is based on three assumptions about the nature of things. First, it operates with regard to the *Principle of Ambiguity*. In the rhetorical world, confusion and lack of clarity are natural states of mind. Order is artificial. And the institutions of order, beginning with law and extending ever wider to encompass all forms of human organization, are rhetorical devices. They exist to guide the individual through interaction with his fellows within the context of a defining structure. The Greeks often debated this cultural phenomenon with particular energy especially with respect to the relationship between law and nature. Which is the stronger? The natural impulses that afflict us all, the emotions and desires and the like? Or the artificial constructions of law and government that seek to channel animal energy into acceptable social forms? Sophists like Protagoras and Gorgias come down on the side of positivism. There is no unchanging reality. Change, in fact, is the only Reality.

That fact leads to a second assumption of rhetoric, the *Principle of Structure*. In the absence of order, any structure will be effective. The more refined and considered it is, of course, the more effective it can be. "Structure" refers to all manner of things, some familiar, others not. Clearly human organizations of all kinds are structures, from baseball teams to corporations. Rhetoric is itself a structuring art. As an art of persuasion its materials are words and images, sentences and paragraphs, arguments and examples, all of which are used to organize the responses and actions of an audience. As an attitude about the world rhetoric underwrites all kinds of processes and methods that aim to produce order out of chaos. Structure is implemented for one end, to warrant the effects of action.

Finally, there is the *Principle of Control*. Its influence is felt across the spectrum of communication, from the invention of proper forms to the execution of actual speech. Modern civilization is preoccupied with control, for it is ever-mindful of the flux and drift of the perpetual change within which it exists. The Principle of Control is essentially Gorgian. It emphasizes timing and opportunity; the provocative phrase misfires if the circumstance is not right, the consummating action is wasted if it comes too soon or too late. The sophist grabs hold of the moment for some particular end, an action, assent, agreement, entertainment, education, pleasure. Control implies consciousness of the acting self, the scene of enactment and the other persons in the play.

The relativistic conception of knowledge, revolutionary in the fifth century B.C., is something that we now take for granted. Our society is based on the three related suppositions that originate with the ancient sophists: that the human being is the arbiter of his own fate, that law and justice are tied to human standards and not to capricious divine forces, and that the individual conscience is the ultimate repository of right and wrong. Protagoras' "man is the measure" summarizes succinctly the basis for change. It encapsulates a theory of moral relativism that philosophers ever since have filled volumes trying to explicate. It accounts for the collapse of central authority, in our time as well as in Protagoras', by putting the individual ahead of the group, the one ahead of the many. And, most important of all, the Protagorean formulation frames the five central assumptions of our time. *Words are tools. Images are real. Information is power. Change is inevitable. Truth is relative.*

These ideas shape our innermost thoughts about living well in a world that depends on technological innovation and the embodiment of theory in *products* as well as in *practice*. They invest our art and literature with the archetypal themes and sophisticated forms and symbols that we use to portray the most rudimentary emotions. They control the processes of decision-making by which we choose the goods we consume, the leaders we follow, the things we study and the opinions we believe or doubt. They give rise to the fundamental concepts and methods of our political, cultural and educational institutions. They are the keystones of our sophistication and, as such, intertwine the present with the past.

Ours is an age of instruments as well as technologies and the two streams flow together. It is commonplace these days to assess things according to their utility, and as a consequence, language has acquired a prosaic, mundane function. Words are tools wielded in the service of often indeterminate ends pursued within the context of shifting circumstances and conflicting needs. We have lost confidence in the intrinsic worth of language as an embodiment of truth *per se*. In our sophistication, we have recognized that more often than not words obscure or shade or distort the thoughts we assume they relay. There is much to the complaint that most problems these days result from the "failure to communicate." Yet that admission is but an excuse masking as a reason. It only scratches the surface of the dilemma, as if a better understanding of the parts of speech or the structures of sentences or the techniques of communication can remedy the situation. It is no accident that ambiguity is now the coin of the realm. Entire industries of interpretation—law, journalism, politics, even religion—have been made necessary and wealthy by the need to clarify the underlying intentions of expression. We know, as the sophists first realized, that an evolving, dynamic language is the instrument of change.

Our conception of language is broader than that of the sophists, and rhetoric reflects the difference. In politics especially, rhetoric is being transformed into a thing quite unanticipated by the sophists of antiquity. For them, after all, public speech was the most important aspect of an active life in community. It was the key to motivating people to act or for dissuading them from action. The Greeks quickly took up the sophistic promise to empower anyone, despite the circumstances of birth or education, to lead the city-state. Now, however, persuasion involves much more than the physical presence of an articulate sophist.

As an art of persuasion, rhetoric is no longer based only in verbal arguments. It is rooted in images and impressions, in the almost exclusively emotional aspects of imitation and pretense. Rhetoric is now concerned with visual appeal. Television, of course, is largely responsible for this transformation. The premium it puts on pictures over words has resulted in the evolution of a new imagistic rhetoric, an art of analysis and articulation that has infiltrated every aspect of social life. We are still struggling with this transformation of the essentially verbal conception of rhetoric into a visual art. It has caused much consternation among those thoughtful souls who attempt to distinguish between image and reality in every realm.

Their efforts are misplaced. In our time, images *are* real. Image is for us what *logos* was for the sophist. It is the communicating symbol, the underlying rationale, the abiding proof, the mutable sign, the physical embodiment of an idea or emotion or impulse. Corporations pay great sums to the practitioners of imagistic rhetoric to invent fetching, appealing, communicating "logos" for their companies and their products. Our sophists descend directly from Gorgias of Leontini and Protagoras of Abdera who would subscribe to the modern expression of an ancient idea that "since all human inquiry moves within the realm of opinion, where deception is easy, *all persuasion is the result of the force of eloquence rather than rational insight.*" The image is the most articulate force. It is reality itself.

Information is power. Words are tools. Images are real. Change is inevitable. Truth is relative. These are the modern manifestations of the rhetorical probability invented by Corax and Tisias, the rhetorical opportunity devised by Gorgias, and the rhetorical relativism espoused by Protagoras. Pushed to extremes, they produce two opposed statements of reality. Each is valid in its own terms. Neither subsumes the other. Both enjoy long, complex histories of development and interaction. Both operate in the modern world. Fitted with a sophisticated mode of inquiry, analysis and judgment, these statements can be elaborated into elegantly structured epistemologies. Between the poles of their extremes we can invent all the systematic philosophies of Western civilization. Treated as separate starting points for discussion and debate, they become the commonplaces of sophisticated rhetoric. In short, these common assumptions ground an existence caught up in the flow of perpetual change. They support two distinct intellectual tendencies.

On one hand, we subscribe to the notion that *things are never what they seem to be*. The world is like an onion composed of layers of illusions each created consciously for some purpose. The veil of language obscures the truth. It must be pierced in order to reveal the underlying substantial nature of things. Reality resides beneath or beyond or above the surface. Knowledge of it is attained by special methods and sciences. Since we symbolize our thoughts in order to persuade others to think and act as we do, we employ technical arts of linguistic analysis—semantics and rhetoric and logic—to discover the substance behind every statement. "Telling" and "acting" are distinct from "knowing." Wisdom and eloquence call upon different arts for their realization. This is the psychology of self-doubt and it produces the organized sciences that aim to uncover hidden truths through systematic investigation, evaluation and judgment.

On the other hand, we also believe that *things are only what they seem to be*. The world is a vast, variegated, endlessly intriguing, undulating surface. Society is a construction of impressions and images, the only constituents of all that there is to know. It is an epistemology of the word, the image, and the intention. The mask of language is reality itself. We create reality by making claims about it, by asserting and proving that one thing is true and that another is not. Eloquence is the art of arts through which wisdom comes into play. As a result, the realms of communal action—politics, business and education—have become vastly complicated confidence games. They run on heavy doses of positive thinking and self-confidence. They depend on our ability to invent the whole scheme and fabric of modern life: the images, rationalizations, arguments, explanations, symbolic systems, complex social organizations, and political myths that constitute in their totality our culture. This view of things animates every act of self-assertion. It also produces the arts of manipulation that create the apparent realities we consider necessary to the efficient operation of complex society.

In practice, we are always running between the two camps. At the most elementary level, we subscribe to the first statement in order to explain failure or consequences that are unacceptable. We proclaim the second when our vision wins the competition with other views. Success, after all, is its own proof of validity. In both cases, it is the *seeming to be* that matters, for rhetoric is the art of appearances. At the most sophisticated level, these statements embody the paradoxical impulses of our times. When rhetoric is grounded in self-doubt, it serves as a method of analysis to reveal motives and intentions beneath the surface of language. It is the foundation of *skepticism*. When rhetoric is grounded in self-confidence, it becomes an art of articulation that creates the verbal reality, however transient, governing common action. It is the basis of *sophistry*. The dialectical tension between self-doubt and self-confidence engages what a Greek would recognize as the paradox between appearance and reality. What is real and what is merely the image? The question revolves around other ancient puzzles that still vex the mind. What do we know? How do we know that we know? How can we tell what we know to others? In an age of sophistication, *seeming to be* is as good as *being* itself. And although they appear to be contrary attitudes, skepticism and sophistry originate in the same phenomenon of social life.

We possess the power to invent *contingent verisimilitudes*, temporary functional realities that are based on what we can agree upon at any given moment. These can be literal representations of a belief that things are what they seem to be. Or they can be intellectual Trojan horses, ostensible gifts of meaning seemingly constructed for one purpose but actually serving another, within which we hide our true intentions. Things are never what they seem to be.

Verisimilitude means "having the appearance of the truth" and encompasses the realm of the probable and the likely. Consequently, it belongs to those class of things treated by rhetoric. As a term of art, it enjoys a long history in literary criticism where it refers to the self-contained believability or likelihood of plot, character, dialogue, scene and thought, all of which are conveyed by words and images. We judge the fictions of literature and art by how well these parts are arranged and expressed. Their true being is thus a kind of beauty, whether it is manifested in form and content or by reference to some assumed standard of functionality, performance or execution.

Broadening the notion of verisimilitude to include social phenomena as well as artistic creations is useful to anyone who would study deceit and deception. It is tempting to focus on clear instances of lying by politicians, publicists and others who seek to manipulate public opinion in an effort to determine its effects on the collective well-being of something called the "public mind." But that communal mind is a tissue of fabrication and prejudiced representation. It is an artwork itself. Indeed, the study of deception is its own contingent verisimilitude. The concept of the public mind encompasses no one, clearly defined thing but is merely a convenient way of looking at the world, a metaphor for group awareness (whatever that may be) on the largest scale. Which public? Whose mind? Gorgias and Protagoras operate with a surer sense of the potentialities and problems of common sense and the public mind. For them, belief is a self-fulfilling truth. Adherence to it by a wider audience is the goal of politics. It is an attitude implicitly understood by the contemporary politician, for the public mind is that which emerges in the opinion polls and from the vote.

The contingent verisimilitude also encompasses life's "vital lies," those mundane misrepresentations we concoct to keep ourselves from being overcome by anxiety, fear, rage and even love. It is a mechanism of control, social as well as personal. It is not so much that we construct our contingent verisimilitudes to avoid something as to condition how that thing, an emotion or opinion or belief or role, can be played in the setting of other minds.

It is this sense of conscious play, of pretense and imitation, that casts verisimilitude as an aesthetic quality rather than as a moral principle. It is what makes science fiction plausible, historical drama acceptable, and some television programs tolerable. The contingent verisimilitudes of everyday life, like the artifacts of art and literature, are products of the mind but are not the mind itself. They are the artificial constructions that we devise and set loose in the effort to make sense of the inarticulate buzz of an ever-changing social world. They are rooted not only in probability but also in relativism; their power to frame the mind's apprehension of its circumstances is completely self-contained. Consequently, they are both the products and process of rhetoric.

In a technical sense, rhetorical verisimilitude refers to the self-defining truthfulness of arguments, examples and other kinds of evidence. It is the ineffable "hanging together" of claims and proofs that convinces an audience to accept something that lacks self-evident veracity, such as the kind of arguments from probability that Corax and Tisias introduced into legal reasoning. In a general sense, rhetorical verisimilitude refers to the state of mind that can be induced in order to accomplish some end. It is the gravitational center of Gorgias' "right moment in time." Our lived verisimilitudes, the minor truths and temporary conditions by which we negotiate success and failure on a daily basis, are *contingent* because they require our acceptance of them. They hold as long as our faith in them can be maintained. They collapse when we change our minds. They are at once public and private, for we create them to explain the world to ourselves as well as to others.

Although the contingent verisimilitude appeals to emotion first and only secondarily to reason, it is in every sense a rationalization. It contains its own inner logic that may not measure up to the more stringent requirements of formal proofs, much as the movie about fictional events long ago in a galaxy far away still works for us as a construction because it holds true to its own terms. The contingent verisimilitude is the basis for community and collaboration. As movie-goers we identify with the plight of the fictional characters and accept their world as our own, at least for the length of the film. As members of a rhetorically determined community, we participate in the contingent verisimilitudes of politics and history that frame at any one moment what we understand to be our culture.

Conversely, individual identity is also a product of the contingent verisimilitude, for our net worth as citizens of polity and heirs of tradition defines us to ourselves as well as to others. In every instance, the contingent verisimilitude is the basis of an aesthetic view of life that dominates all others—the moral, scientific, technological, theological and ideological. It becomes the only foundation for judgment in a world constructed on image and impression, emotion and belief.

Thus, the motivating rhetorical impulses of modern life transcend the technical requirements of a verbal art to become the art of living in an ever-changing world. Expression assumes a broader meaning in our time. It encompasses not only utterance in words, but also the embodiment of ideas, emotions, concepts, thoughts and attitudes in visual, verbal and imagistic forms. Expression may be symbolic and representational or mimetic and literal, as modern advertising shows by the range of its rhetorical vocabulary. Or it may be institutional and structural, as in the hierarchical organizations of government, education and business and in the processes, policies and procedures of the modern bureaucracy. Whatever its incarnation, suasive expression is systematic but ephemeral. It guides the artistic forms peculiar to our times, videos and movies and the like. It also informs the structured organizations that make communal action possible in a technologically based society.

A life spent seeming to be is an artistic creation of the first order. Like all artifacts of the mind it too is open to interpretation and judgment, comprehension and misunderstanding. Matters would be simpler perhaps if things were only as they seemed to be. Life could be lived on the surface of the sensed world in confidence and with self-assurance or, failing that, with fatalism and resignation. Before the fifth century B.C. human beings could put their trust in the invisible natural forces that shaped the earth or in the imagined potent deities that populated the public mind of the time. But Gorgias and Protagoras and others like them started us on a journey into precincts of the human mind where the power of self-determination lay waiting to be discovered and exercised. What came before them was innocence and naivete. They left in their wake a sophistication that forever altered our ability to believe so willingly in mythic forces. We are only now realizing the implications of their in-novations. Our powerful information technologies and com-munication tools magnify tenfold the capabilities of the individual mind and give it room to play unknown in ancient times. The idea of rhetoric that has evolved from these early speculations is a uniquely self-conscious art. Indeed, rhetorical self-consciousness is the well-spring of the inventions by which we seek to alter the form and function of the material world and to order and direct the social realm.

The interplay between skepticism's all encompassing doubt and sophistry's unquestioning confidence now paradoxically defines the relationship between individuals and communities. It determines what constitutes knowledge and how it ought to be taught. And it delineates the lines of power between and among individuals, institutions and society. Rhetorical principles infuse history, politics, education and ethics. They determine their characteristic contents, mandate their idiosyncratic forms and compel the communal pursuit of their pragmatic ends.

The shifting boundaries between individual being and social character not only determine the present quality of life in com-munity, they also describe by their fluctuations and readjust-ments how human beings view the nature of their progress, from credulous naiveté to potent sophistication. Among the legacies of the Greeks none has proven more enduring and influential than the invention of history; not the technical disci-pline that is now the preserve of professional historians but the attitude toward the past that allows each one of us to create the present and influence the future.

So regarded, history is a kind of "seeming to be" that con-tributes to the viability of culture. It is a product of the mind's search for validation. As such, history occupies a paradoxical position in the operation of modern culture. The pervasive present-mindedness of sophistication masks an underlying preoccupation with the past. For the sophist's way of knowing eventually centers on the history of each and every individual mind that gropes for self-enlightenment and self-knowledge amid the confusion of an ever changing present. But the idiosyncratic and unique history of the individual is understandable only in the context of the political, educational, and ethical circumstances that express the many manifestations of self-consciousness. The intricate relationship between individual being and social character describes in its fullness and complexity the present paradox of self-knowledge. Our search for the self is connected at every point with the larger quest for our collective origins. Answering the question "Who am I?" entails the conscientious pursuit of the inquiry "Who are we?" To know one's self is to know our collective selves.

CHAPTER TWO

Inventing the Past:
The Purpose of History
in a Sophisticated Age

A historian is a prophet in reverse.
—Friedrich Schlegel

T HE RISE OF RHETORICAL SELF-CONSCIOUSNESS in the fifth century
B.C. was accompanied by a reconstituting of history around
the power of human beings, rather than supernatural
forces, to determine human destiny. This notion of history persists into our own sophisticated age, enlivening a variety of
activities seemingly far removed from either the efforts of ancient historians or the speculations of contemporary academicians. Our uses of history reflect the early innovations of
antiquity, particularly the framing of contemporary events within
some larger picture of the evolution of human society from
simplicity to sophistication. Consciousness of the self, after all,
entails awareness of the nurturing environment that produces
self-consciousness. We construct intricate genealogies for ourselves, as individuals and as a people, in order to validate the
pervasive present-mindedness that dominates everyday life.
Even academic history, which is a relatively recent invention,
reflects the desire to sophisticate the search for the past, to
provide it with an appropriate and potent terminology, and to
harness it in the service of self-improvement as well as self-

knowledge. It betrays, that is, our primal need to make a science of life.

As an intellectual activity, however, historical thinking began long before sophistic thought asserted itself. It first surfaced in the form of myths, epic tales and records of local heroes and events. Different though these early accounts were in form and content, all dealt with the problem of how man came to be as he is. From the start, history has been a search after the primordial roots of the present. In its early mythic forms, history was directed to abstract matters such as the nature of mortal existence, the genesis of the gods and the origins of the cosmos. With the onset of sophistic thought, however, this search came to be concerned with the nature of the human being as a thoughtful, self-motivated, individual entity, and as a social creature. By the time of Protagoras and Gorgias, the ancient myths could no longer support the method or purpose of the inquiry. The sophisticated mind sought terrestrial explanations for mundane events in the motives and consequences of human action.

The mythic tradition had provided a necessary continuity for life that linked humanity not only to the past but to nature and the gods. But because myth is at once concrete, allusive, vivid, symbolic and associative, it relies on a collective consciousness that subordinates individual minds to the power of archetypal forces. Communities of interpretation arise to address its more problematic aspects, to construct a sense of purpose for it, to trace its genealogies and theogenies, and to induce an order that is at once self-explanatory and mysterious. The structure, function and ends of mythology require a priestly class to interpret its ambiguities and to harness its archaic powers. The process is by nature exclusive, mystical and undemocratic. When mythic history was first attacked in the late sixth century B.C. by the natural philosophers in the Greek settlements in Western Asia, it was on the grounds not of accuracy about the events it reported but as a view of life in the cosmos, as the story of divine intervention and the history of the gods. The natural scientists looked for other causes to explain generation, growth, decay and death. To the emerging sophisticated minds of ancient Greece, mythology was more religion than explanation, more mental slavery than intellectual illumination.

Mythic history attempted to order the events of the past within a framework of self-centered, self-referential causes and effects that ultimately accounted for all things known. Sophistic thinkers, however, tended to make the past what they wished it to be through a discriminating rather than a comprehensive approach to historical analysis. History was at best a myth agreed upon, with the emphasis on the "agreed upon." It was a serviceable, flexible, adaptable concoction, open to changes and amendments that suit the immediate requirements of persuasion and belief. When, for example, a thinker like Protagoras articulates a creation myth, one that is later embroidered upon by Plato for his own purposes, it is to account for the progress of human beings from brute animals to civilized city dwellers. It expressed in pleasing, allusive literary form the rise of sophistic epistemology and its presumption of the inherent powers of the human mind. The Protagorean creation myth is a paradoxical explanation of human history because it engages the form of a divinely inspired, mythic explanation to transmit the substance of a uniquely human invention. It links the radical epistemology of sophistic to the familiar ontology of myth. It is argument masquerading as revelation. In the markets and meeting places of ancient Greece, historical analysis buttressed the objectives of debate and public performances of all kinds.

Myths began to be interpreted for their metaphorical qualities rather than their literal content. Mythology became literature much as the Bible is now studied as an artificial, human construction noteworthy for its verbal devices, rhetorical structures and linguistic inventions. The sophistication of mythology removed the certainties inherent in the cosmic explanation of divine and human existence. As a result, there was no substantial reality called the "past." Rather, the history of communities was propagated and refined in the context of many written and oral forms that evolved according to the circumstances of motivated interpretations. Mythic history was grounded in and served the emotions. Beginning with the sophists, however, the facts of past events and the statements of mortal predecessors began to figure into historic accounts. The line of descent of the ancient historians from Herodotus to Thucydides, Xenophon and, later, Polybius is marked by a progressive abandonment of mythic tales and constructions. History becomes the self-consciously researched and constructed invention of sophisticated minds. Its importance is tied to the uses that could be made of it in the present and the implications it bore for the future.

From Thucydides and his invented speeches, dialogues and debates at the end of the fifth century B.C. to Plutarch and his invented lives in the second century A.D., ancient sophistic historians aimed at something greater than mere preservation, annotation, cataloguing and commentary. They sought to locate the concrete reality of life as it is expressed by historical events or embodied in historical personages within patterns that could be analyzed and understood, interpreted and judged, imitated or avoided. Both Thucydides and Plutarch understood the effects of individual character and personality on the unfolding of cultural history. Both conceived of history as powered by the tension between the arbitrary actions of powerful persons and the irresistible forces of historical inevitability. Both pursued their art of history self-consciously and with a great regard for aesthetic values. Finally, both exemplify the idea that a historian is a prophet in reverse. They are explainers of the past who labored for present utility as well as for the benefit of unborn generations. Thucydides dedicates his work to the future, to us, so that we may imitate its methods and engage its patterns to analyze our own state of affairs. Thucydidean history demands our participation and contemplation. Plutarch provides character analysis that can serve as the basis of imitation for moral edification so that we might discover from the examples of great men who lived in the past how to best order our lives in the present. Thucydides and Plutarch represent two streams of sophistic thought that flow into our own conception of history as a cultural phenomenon that shapes our social character and as a personal experience that determines individual being.

Thucydides (c. 460–399 B.C.) lived through the flowering, fruition and decline of Classical Greece. He was an Athenian who traced his ancestry to Thrace, in northern Greece, where his family apparently owned an estate situated near the important gold and silver mines at Mount Pangaeum. The proximity probably accounts for the wealth that allowed him to pursue his task of writing the "history of the war fought between Athens and Sparta." He was a man of some foresight and fortitude, for he recognized early in the conflict that it "was going to be a great war and more worth writing about than any of those which had taken place in the past." In fact, it was to last 27 years, from 431–404 B.C., interrupted only by the uneasy Peace of Nicias (421–414 B.C.). The war Thucydides set out to describe eventually enveloped the Hellenic world and led not only to the downfall of Athens but also to the collapse of the city-state as a dynamic political entity.

Thucydides writes as both a participant and a knowledge-able observer. His work is filled with details about people, battles, revolutions, debates and myriad other events that transpired in widely separated theaters of the conflict. He served in the war as one of Athens' ten annually elected generals. Because of his Thracian origins he was given command in 424 of the city's fleet in the northern Aegean Sea, a strategic and important area of the Athenian Empire across which ran the vital supply lines from the Black Sea granaries that fed Athens. It was in this role that he incurred the wrath of the Athenians who blamed him for the loss to the Spartans of the most important city in the region, Amphipolis. The evidence that comes down to us is mixed but it indicates a certain tardiness in dispatching his triremes during the course of battle. Rightly or wrongly, he was banished from Athens and not allowed to return until 404, after the war had ended in the Athenian defeat and a general amnesty had been declared. He spent many of the intervening years in Spartan territory and so is able to relate developments on both sides of the conflict. He also maintained a private network of contacts and correspondents throughout the Greek world, people who like himself were aristocratic members of the *intelligentsia* in their respective city-states. Thus, he was able to gather much information from a wide variety of sources. He worked on his history throughout his exile and was probably in the process of finishing and refining it when he died around 399 B.C. His *History of the Peloponnesian War* breaks off in mid-sentence, discussing events of 411, the 21st year of warfare.

Thucydides' work has controlled how subsequent generations have thought about the war. Though his account is comprehensive on a grand scale, he appears to omit much that has been subsequently discovered through careful research and analysis of other sources. As many scholars have pointed out, he exercises a peculiar and highly refined sense of selection in the materials he chooses to report. Thucydides has spawned a scholarly industry of analysis and commentary that seizes upon his omissions and inclusions as evidence for his intentions and designs. The resulting judgments of his work are contradictory and often say more about the underlying prejudices and predilections of the scholarly commentator than they do about Thucydides. He has been hailed as the greatest historian of all time, and as the worst. Some call him a pseudo-dramatist, others a moralist. His method of analysis has been criticized as haphazard and unhistorical at the same time his thought and expression have been praised for their novelty, inventiveness and penetration. He has been assaulted for his biases and prejudices, castigated for his inaccuracies and inventions, berated for his rejection of documentary proof and source materials, and pitied for the awesomeness of a task that some think he ultimately failed to perform. Some have accepted his conclusions and rejected his methods. Others laud his innovations in historical methodology and reject his judgments. Through it all, his work emerges as the foremost example of the uses that can be made of history in a sophisticated age. It embodies the pragmatic methods and paradoxical consequences that are the hallmark of sophistic thought. He is the first sophistic historian.

Thucydides' triumph lies in his invention of the idea that the disparate events that occurred between 431 and 404 B.C. constitute a single, vast and complex movement in human history, the transformation of civilization itself. He saw what eluded others, that his own turbulent times were a turning point in the progress of the Greeks from simplicity to sophistication. He created an explanation of the period that was made up of concrete events but which drew its significance from the interpretations he put on them. So doing, he self-consciously passes to us a vision of how things came to be as they are. He invents the past by creating a history to support his perception of a wider, more intricate and ultimately more destructive conflict than even his ruined contemporaries realized. He set out to teach a fundamental lesson about power, empire and the corruptibility of the human being.

Even with this purpose, however, Thucydides is no moralizing intellectual. Like the sophists with whom he shared an underlying confidence in the creative power of the mind, he focuses primarily on specific actions to communicate general principles. His technique of describing in detail particular events in order to reveal their universal importance embodies the sophistic epistemology. He developed a systematic approach to investigate the causes, motives and circumstances behind events. In many instances, Thucydides states the ostensible reasons for a decision or policy, such as the violation of commonly accepted religious or ancestral claims, then delves into the actual political or social background that gave rise to the dispute in the first place. It is a brilliant technique for revealing that things are never as they seem to be in war and politics, though the speeches of generals and politicians may argue that matters are as simple and compelling as they appear. Within the text of Thucydides, then, skepticism and sophistry are arrayed in such fashion and to such purposes that the causes of the war are explored and exposed in all their intricacy.

Like the physician of his day, Thucydides' purpose is diagnosis and prognosis. He looks for the "exciting cause" to explain the outbreak of war and finds it in the inevitable, paradoxical demands of imperial ambition. His history is written for those who desire a knowledge of the past as an aid for the preparation of the future. The task requires a hermeneutics of history grounded in the assumptions and operations of sophistic rhetoric. Thucydides was keenly aware of the paradoxical nature of thought and expression, of the capacity of the mind to justify itself through the manipulation of words and images. He himself engages the process of justification, for his history is one vast rhetorical exercise that simultaneously details and embodies the sophistication of politics, language and culture. It can only be measured against the demands of rhetoric for argument and persuasion. Historical justification exists as a kind of "seeming to be" that draws its veracity from the ideas and conceptions we use to order the events that transpire around us. In a passage as powerful and penetrating as anything written on the relationship between politics and language Thucydides details the linguistic novelties and duplicities, the double speak of his day, that were forced to the surface by the irrationality of the war.

> So revolutions broke out in city after city, and in places where the revolutions occurred late the knowledge of what had happened previously in other places caused still new extravagances of revolutionary zeal, expressed by an elaboration in the methods of seizing power and by unheard-of atrocities in revenge. To fit in with the change of events, words, too, had to change their usual meanings. What used to be described as a thoughtless act of aggression was now regarded as the courage one would expect to find in a party member. To think of the future and wait was merely another way of saying one was a coward. Any idea of moderation was just an attempt to disguise one's unmanly character. Ability to understand a question from all sides meant that one was totally unfitted for action. Fanatical enthusiasm was the mark of a real man, and to plot against an enemy behind his back was perfectly legitimate self-defense. Anyone who held violent opinions could always be trusted, and anyone who objected became suspect . . . . As a result of these revolutions, there was a general deterioration of character throughout the Greek world. The simple way of looking at things, which is so much the mark of a noble nature, was regarded as ridiculous and soon ceased to exist. (III.82)

These revolutions overturned more than established political regimes. They also destroyed the basis of community itself. The Greek *polis*, or city-state, was constructed around ideas and methods of government that were rooted in simple notions about the relationships between human beings. Thucydides' history is more than a story of war as a series of battles or alliances or temporary truces. For him, the *idea* of the Peloponnesian War has a wider sense. It is not simply a sequence of events described chronologically. It is a cultural

artwork of the largest kind, one that portrays not only victory
and defeat but also moral breakdown, social reorganization, the
collapse of central authority and the transformation of Athenian
society itself. Thucydides illuminates the process of cultural
change through many dramatic devices, most notably the recreation of speeches, diplomatic debates and in one instance a
fictional dialogue between Athenian and Melian negotiators.
These aspects of his history have drawn the fire of professional
historians ever since who would prefer verbatim accounts and,
whenever possible, actual transcripts from the discussions
themselves. Thucydides' inventions may seem to be the equivalent of the contemporary dramatic recreation of news events.
The debate about their historical veracity often resembles the
argument over the modern practice of simulating the news. Yet
they are the perfect vehicles for the sophistic historian intent on
revealing the complex moral and psychological issues that animate the war. It is the mind of Thucydides, after all, and not
some objective historical force, that compels *The Peloponnesian
War* to unfold as it does. Its significance for us is rhetorical, not
historical.

Thucydides recognized better than anyone that Greek culture had moved irreversibly from simplicity to sophistication.
He reveals the progressive effects of sophistic thinking on the
relationship between power, politics and personal character. In
many respects, the democratic social order contained the seeds
of its own destruction. Its culture of legal and political equality,
freedom, personal empowerment and sophistic education set
loose powerful social forces that could at first be controlled by
rational leadership. The triumph of Pericles was his ability to
balance the internal dynamics of Athens with the external
requirements of a maritime empire to produce a self-renewing
society. But the very virtues of sophistic thought that make
possible democratic society ultimately weaken the basis for
communal action. Inherently unstable and open to reversals of
policy and practice, Athenian democracy fell victim during the
war to accidents of nature, such as the plague and the death of
Pericles, that induced a kind of mass irrationality. In the volatile
environment of sophisticated politics, words lose their meaning,

once noble attitudes are regarded as base and cowardly, tradition is despised, and guile and deception replace straight talk as the principal means of communication. The many invented speeches, diplomatic exchanges and conversations Thucydides reports are intended to show that in a world controlled by relativity, opportunism and probability, there is no basis for trust. Suspicion and distemper united with hubris and cleverness at crucial times during the war to produce missed opportunities, false peace, stupid strategies and disastrous policies.

As an aesthetic creation, *The Peloponnesian War* represents Thucydides' formal solution to a vexing problem: how to portray the manifold ethical dilemma of sophisticated Greece in a form that compensates for the limitations of poetry and mythic history. His work is a conscious construction that defines and applies its own unique interpretative science grounded in rhetoric. As such, the work offers "better evidence than that of the poets, who exaggerate the importance of their themes, or of the prose chroniclers, who are less interested in telling the truth than in catching the attention of their public, whose authorities cannot be checked, and whose subject matter (owing to the passage of time) is mostly lost in the unreliable streams of mythology."

Thucydides' history investigates and interprets the nature of sophisticated democratic politics. The war between Athens and Sparta is transformed at every stage into an opposition between liberal expansionism and conservative contraction, political innovation and political stagnation, moral relativity and traditional authority. The spread of sophistic thought unleashed social forces which operated paradoxically, for the Athenian experience with democratic politics was a source of creativity as well as destruction. The contrasting views of Sparta and Athens that Thucydides develops throughout his history often show the degradation of politics as an art of living in community. Both cities, as well as their many allies and thralls, are inexorably affected by the war. Politics no longer operates as a form of self-expression. Its processes and institutions no longer assure self-restraint. Instead, the sophistic innovations in speech and government transform politics into a form of public display and make rhetoric merely an art of manipulation. Self-promotion, self-indulgence and self-importance replace the idea of the *polis* as the ultimate expression of political character.

Aesthetics and political science come together in Thucydides to offer a solution to the perceived disruption between public performance and private intentions, social character and individual being. In form and content, *The Peloponnesian War* is a response to sophistication that seeks to avoid, on one hand, the retreat to idealized reason that will be Plato's reaction to politics in the next century and, on the other, the cynical play on the passions that was the sophists' in the last. The death of the *polis* carried with it the demise of a form of individual being that found expression in the old politics, the ancient certainties and the traditional ways of coming to know. The fragmented world of sophistic epistemology, where each person becomes the center of all that can be known and acted upon, is by nature chaotic and ambiguous. Its dangers are depicted in the story of the Athenians who, though they were powerful and inventive, had good reason for caution and self-discipline. In less than fifty years they passed from empire to enslavement. To address the new circumstances, Thucydides proposes a new science of historical interpretation. As a navigational art it can serve to remind the individual, through the specific lessons of a universalized history, that his interests are validated by responsible action pursued on behalf of the larger community.

In the paradoxical example of Thucydides we discover the uses of history in a sophisticated age. He employs the devices of sophisticated rhetoric to investigate and interpret the dangers of sophisticated politics. In the end, he produces a sophisticated history that is of lasting value, not because we are doomed to repeat the particular folly of the Athenians but because we can apply the universal method of Thucydides to evaluate our own experiences as individuals and as members of a wider community. Our understanding of his method and ends, in turn, derives from the aesthetic power of his work. Thucydides draws the reader into the narrative, binds him to the interests of his characters, raises in him the same concerns and fears that afflict them, disillusions him as to the real causes of their downfall, and leaves him to ponder the foolishness of their ways. "It will be enough for me," he writes, "if these words of mine are judged useful by those who want to understand clearly the events which happened in the past and which (human nature being what it is) will be repeated in the future." In the end, *The Peloponnesian War* is Thucydides' solution to the ancient questions. What do we know? How do we know that we know? How do we tell others what we know?

The example of Thucydides illuminates the epistemological relationship between sophistic history and rhetoric. Sophistic history is rhetorical because it is an interpretive activity motivated by an overarching desire to order the world for some purpose. It seeks to discover in the personages and events of the past those key terms, concepts, ideas, and patterns of thought and action that can be useful in the present. Since interpretation serves a purpose (it is an intentional act exercised in specific circumstances), sophistic history is preparatory. It lays the groundwork for common understanding of past events in order to determine how the present is played out. Finally, sophistic history seeks to resolve the conditions of life that give rise to dissonance, disagreement and disaster. After all, it is a primary assumption of the sophistic historian that clear understanding of the patterns of behavior and the causes of disruption leads to the healing of the division between thought and action. Sophistic history is thus a therapeutic art. Within these three realms of utility the rhetorical concept of "invention" assumes two senses. First, it refers to the actual *creation* of history during the fifth century B.C. as a unique discipline of the mind organized around a characteristic methodology, intention and end. Second, it also refers to the *creativity* of historical thinking as a process for discovering the significance of antecedent events in light of current conditions and future consequences. Thucydides embodies both aspects of history as a means of coming to terms with the past by literally "making history." At heart, his was a poetic art.

So, too, were the biographical inventions of Plutarch (46–125 A.D.), who undertook to reconstruct the lives of famous Romans and Greeks for the entertainment and moral instruction of his audience, an educated class of citizens who appreciated Greek language and culture. Rome was at its zenith in these years, prosperous, powerful and pragmatic. Although Plutarch spent most of his life in the small Greek city of Chaeronea, a place known principally for two famous battles fought near it in antiquity, he also travelled from time to time throughout Greece and Italy. He studied at Athens under Ammonius of Lamptrae, a philosopher and historian of religion. He was apparently sent to Rome on official city business sometime in his early adulthood and returned there between 75–90. Although his primary concerns were the commercial and political fortunes of Chaeronea, he also found time to lecture on rhetoric and philosophy. Consequently, he was exposed to the intellectual circles in Roman life that were intentionally reviving the study of Greek literature and was able to augment his own sophistic education. It was during these visits that he probably collected the materials that would form the basis of his major work, the *Parallel Lives*, for which he is best remembered today.

Plutarch's primary language was Greek and though he spent some time in Rome he apparently never mastered Latin. During the second century A.D. Greek acquired a cachet for cultivation and civilization. It was spoken by the educated classes as a sign of sophistication, much as the Russian nobility spoke French to show their worldliness, taste and civil ambitions. Greek literature and philosophy were studied intently by the sons of the Roman upper classes as a kind of primer for entry into public life. Greek art set the standards for form, style and beauty throughout the empire. By the end of the second century even a Roman emperor, Marcus Aurelius, would commune with himself in Greek. Rome had conquered Greece by force of arms but, in turn, surrendered to all things Greek. The period in which Plutarch wrote heralded the emergence of a new international culture based on a melding of distinctly Grecian and Roman habits of mind, artistic impulses and national characteristics. More than any other figure of his time, Plutarch represents the effects of this culture on the conception of history as a personal experience of the world.

His *Parallel Lives* is constructed around pairings of Greek and Roman statesmen, political leaders, generals and other people of historical importance. Each pair is followed by a brief comparative essay evaluating the strengths and weakness of the lives under analysis. Sometimes these lives are truly parallel, reflecting Plutarch's discovery of an essential similarity between two figures separated by culture, time and circumstance. At other times, the lives he details parallel each other in a negative fashion, one virtuous and the other not. Plutarch is mindful of the differences that exist between his paired examples, especially when he treats figures who are uniquely Greek or Roman, for example Alexander the Great and Julius Caesar. Then, the task is to illuminate the traits of character that all great men share despite the different circumstances of their lives. In his work *Political Precepts* Plutarch comments on matters of particular interest to us, such as how politics in the autonomous Greek city-states had changed from the days of the first sophists. "Nowadays, when the affairs of our cities do not admit of military commands or the overthrowing of tyrannies or joint actions with allies," he writes, a young man must pursue other outlets for a public career. "There are still public lawsuits and embassies to the Emperor, demanding a man of ardent disposition but at the same time one of courage and good sense."

In that description we find the essential difference between the uncertain conditions that produced Thucydides and the predictable circumstances that rewarded Plutarch. On the one hand, life in the ancient *polis* was demanding. It required an art of persuasion and power that could move men to act together in common defense and for common interests. Rhetoric served as an instrument of change in the Greece of Pericles and the sophists. It was the basis of political life. By Plutarch's time, rhetoric was subordinated to the imperial realities. Political decision-making was arbitrary. It centered on the personage of the emperor and the institutions of empire. There was not much call for an art that could galvanize the populace into overthrowing a tyrant or organizing a conspiracy of neighboring, like-minded cities. Rhetoric found expression in legal training. "There are still public lawsuits," Plutarch reminds his correspondent, and "embassies to the Emperor." Rhetoric had become an art of presentation and petitioning, an agent of stability that bolstered the nostalgic ruminations of intellectuals. Its practice still demanded a man eloquent enough to be heard. But it also called for one sensible enough to know when to be quiet. The shift in the function of rhetoric thus mirrors a shift in the concepts of propriety and morality that ultimately define the relationship between individual being and social character. It is a movement away from bold assertion and self-empowerment toward affable accommodation and self-effacement. The struggling democracy of warring Greek city-states has been replaced by the secure autocracy of an empire at peace with itself.

Athens had changed greatly in the 600 years between Thucydides and Plutarch. Defeat in the Peloponnesian War eventually led the Athenian oligarchs who assumed power briefly in 404 B.C. to outlaw the sophists and to ban the teaching of rhetoric. Sophistic thought had acquired the odor of radicalism and revolution. By Plutarch's time, Athens had become the center of Greek learning in a stable Roman world. Sophistic thought was harnessed as a mode of validation and self-justification.

Where Thucydides writes political history to interpret the turmoil and strife of a dying Greek civilization, Plutarch writes personal histories to justify the morality and prosperity of a flourishing Roman imperium. The former focuses on the general circumstances within which human beings struggle against each other, and the latter on the specific character of individual men as it is revealed against the backdrop of uncontrollable fate. Plutarch was aware of the differences between history and biography as conscious art forms as well as vehicles for the invention of the past.

> . . . I shall make no other preface than to beg my readers not to complain if I do not tell of all the famous actions of these men, nor even speak exhaustively, but rather that I epitomize them. For it is not histories that I am writing, but lives, and in the most illustrious deeds there is not always a manifestation of virtue or vice. A slight thing like a phrase or a jest often reveals more of a character than battles where thousands fall, or the greatest armaments, or siege of cities. Therefore, just as painters reproduce likenesses in their portraits from the face and the expression of

the eyes, wherein the character shows itself, but do not focus on other parts of the body, so I must be permitted to devote myself to the signs of the soul in men. By means of these I will portray the life of each, leaving to others the description of their great contests. ("Alexander," I.2)

Plutarch draws on two traditions of biography already well established by the time he began to compose his _Parallel Lives_. First, there was the tradition of documenting the lives of the famous and the infamous by reproducing their sayings, anecdotes about their exploits and even apocryphal tales illustrating their manner and disposition. These served either as models for instruction or as cautionary tales about excesses and vices to be avoided. Second, there was also a tradition of collecting biographies that shared a common profession or art, such as philosophers, painters and the like. Plutarch's _Parallel Lives_ falls somewhere between these two traditions of biography. Single characters are treated both as individuals and as types, as idiosyncratic personalities as well as members of common ranks, professions, or avocations.

As an aesthetic invention, the blending of these traditions creates a more dynamic, interactive structure for what had previously been a rather didactic art form. At one level, individual being and social character are interwoven within the tapestry of historical events. At another, similarities and differences between Greek and Roman culture are accented. The interplay between and among these levels of comparison produces in its entirety what can be known about the emerging Graeco-Roman culture. Virtues such as courage, justice, temperance, and prudence are drawn out and examined by reference to men of similar accomplishments or fates. Theseus, the founder of the Athenian polis, is placed along side Romulus, the father of the Roman state. Alexander, the conqueror of Persia and Asia is matched with Caesar, the subduer of Gaul and Europe. Demosthenes, the last voice of democratic Athens is compared with Cicero, the last orator of republican Rome. Plutarch's book cultivates both an understanding of individual character and an awareness of the historical roots for its cultural expression. He invents a past and populates it with people who embody the transition from simplicity to sophistication. He does so, however, not as a sociologist interested in the nature and operation of human communities but as a moralist concerned with the education of right thinking and the execution of right action.

> ... and so our intellectual vision must be applied to such objects which, when contemplated by the mind, delight it and invite it to reach its own proper good. Such objects consist of virtuous deeds. When the mind of the reader has clearly perceived them it is filled with an eager desire to imitate them. ("Pericles," I.3)

A complex psychology enlivens this notion of imitation. It is based on philosophical concepts that still find a place in our view of the matter—intellectual vision, the mind, delight, inspiration, proper good, virtuous deeds, and eager desire. And it is founded on a corollary confidence in the existence of substantial moral values. His is not simply a biography of praise or blame aimed at pleasing an immediate audience. Rather, the *Lives* is a sophisticated attempt to analyze, identify and isolate a unique "moral good [that] creates a stir of activity towards itself and immediately inspires an impulse to practice it in the spectator. This forms his mind and character, not simply by a mere imitation that we look at, but because his investigation of it enables him to acquire a moral purpose." Imitation encompasses the patterns of choice that emerge from our analysis of great men and their deeds. It leads to the discovery of the "fitting" and the "proper," two concepts of rhetoric that Plutarch applies to the art of living. Our study of the historical characters of the past can help us conduct our lives in such a manner that we reproduce their virtues without necessarily reproducing their actions.

Plutarch's invention of the past is an aesthetic creation of the highest order. He often draws analogies between his art and that of the portrait painter. It is no mean comparison, for it reflects his appreciation for the nature of his task. Do not expect an exact rendition of his characters, he warns us. Not only is that impossible, given the span of years that separates him from his subjects, it is also undesirable. Plutarch's purpose of moral instruction requires a subtler, more artistic principle of selection.

> We demand of the artist who paints a portrait of someone beautiful neither to omit entirely any slight blemish that may show nor yet to produce it exactly. The exact reproduction makes the appearance ugly and the omission prevents the likeness from being a true one. In a similar way, since it is difficult, if not impossible, to represent a man's life as stainless and pure, in all that is excellent we must follow the truth exactly and give it fully as if it were his true likeness. Any lapses that occur, however, through human passions or political necessities, we may regard rather as the shortcomings in a particular virtue than as the natural effects of moral baseness. We must treat them as though we were defending human nature, which produces no character perfectly good and indisputably set towards virtue. ("Cimon," II.4)

Paradoxically, valiant deeds and heroic actions alone do not deserve respect. The inclination of human nature to imperfection does for it afflicts us all, noble and base alike, and sets the limits of imitation that Plutarch investigates and exposes in his *Lives*.

Like Thucydides, Plutarch has suffered at the hands of subsequent commentators who fault him for all manner of offenses and omissions. He makes too many digressions, some argue, as if he were a museum tour guide for whom every piece of art offers an occasion for unnecessary reflection. Others complain that we are unable to evaluate his sources and he is too trusting of the likes of Thucydides, who has since been proven wrong. When he criticizes a source it is usually on moral rather than on factual or historical grounds. Still others lament the lack of a clear chronology in his *Lives*. Cicero is the neighbor in time of Demosthenes, Caesar reigns the day after Alexander. Moreover, politics is a mystery to him. He is content to report hearsay and fable without considering the complex circumstances behind the rise or fall, the virtues or vices, of his subjects. Finally, there is little sense of development in his biographies. It is as if his characters spring to life, like Athena from Zeus' brow, full grown and armed with developed personalities and habits.

We can admit the faults and avoid the conclusion, however, that Plutarch is an untrustworthy source, either of information about antiquity or inspiration for our own invention of the past. The opposite is true. His faults are the virtues of sophistic invention. He exemplifies the personal dimension of the uses of history in a sophisticated age. Like Thucydides, Plutarch both embodies and practices a characteristic form of sophistic history. His invention of the past is a rhetorical exercise conditioned by three goals. First, the examination of past examples, some complementary and some contradictory, prepares the grounds for a common understanding about the nature of right and wrong. Second, the interpretation of the actions and statements of famous people lays the foundation for a moral system suited to the conditions of modernity. Finally, examination and interpretation aim to correct aberrant behavior and to inspire proper conduct. In Plutarch, we find all three intentions at work under the rubric of moral instruction, as necessary preconditions for the imitation of attitudes and patterns of choice. The approach is plausible for Plutarch because he writes in an age when individual being and social character unite in public performance. "Doing" is "being" in a sophisticated age. And in the Roman imperium, doing well was a cultural determination based on the merger of two distinct civilizations. Plutarch's *Parallel Lives* serves as the basis for an emerging Graeco-Roman culture that entails its own concept of individual being.

The parallel contributions of Thucydides, the preeminent outsider, and Plutarch, the consummate insider, represent two streams of sophistic history that mold our conception and exercise of historical thinking. On one hand, history is a cultural phenomenon that shapes our social character. On the other, it is a personal experience that determines individual being. In both cases, history is a search after causes that works backwards from observable effects. Thucydides examines the events of the war to discover its motivations. Plutarch examines actions of famous men to discern moral qualities or defects common to us all. Both begin with the presumption that things are never as they seem. Both participate in rhetorical invention as "discovery." There is an essential skepticism in their art that leads each to uncover the hidden patterns of political or personal history. They also devise new verbal forms, structures, and vocabularies appropriate to the products of their discovery. Both develop a complex notion of imitation. At one level, they provide a method of analysis and interpretation that we can imitate to yield specific results to our own invention of the past. At another, each produces qualities of character in action that can serve as the model for moral choices we may face in the future. Ultimately, both are concerned with the dimensions of character, either as the attribute of a people, as in the case of Thucydides, or as the expression of individual being, as we find in Plutarch. Consequently, they represent the two poles of focus that control how we come to terms with ourselves, as individuals as well as a vibrant, inventive culture.

Thucydides writes sophisticated history at the close of the fifth century B.C. He discovers in the opportunism and relativity of Athenian culture the roots of inevitability for the war. They express the flawed character of the Athenians who, without the strong hand of Pericles, give free rein to their ambition, pride and greed. Plutarch writes sophisticated biography at the beginning of the second century A.D. He discovers in the opportunism and relativity of individual men the universal traits that can constitute moral character for each of us, despite the innate weakness and imperfection of the human being. For him, a man's character is his fate. Despite the difference in their subject matter, scope and method, Thucydides and Plutarch exemplify how sophistic history can be grounded in ethical considerations. It is at once preparatory, interpretive and therapeutic.

We, too, are fascinated with the past. Like Thucydides and Plutarch we pursue it in order to give meaning to our own purposes and ambitions. As a form of "seeming to be," sophistic history participates in the psychology of the contingent verisimilitude. It originates in both self-doubt and self-confidence. It is built on belief in human ability, faith in the human intellect, and knowledge of human weakness. It serves as the basis for judgments about right and wrong. It supports decisions calling for action or inaction. It animates and justifies proposed policies and practices. It vindicates the present by rationalizing the past.

The process of making history works at many levels in our time. It is expressed in the works of academic historians who, for all their pretense of objectivity and scientific method, practice a highly sophisticated form of Thucydides' and Plutarch's poetic, rhetorical art. Facts alone do not support conclusions. Historians must also fashion them into a plausible story. They must win an audience through the application of rhetorical aesthetics, for history requires our participation and adherence. Academic history has become irrelevant to daily life. It has been condemned to a place among the disciplines of knowledge and is segregated from the arts of action, all with the connivance of the academicians themselves. It is routinely ignored by those in positions of power and influence. Or, it is twisted grotesquely to fit the preconceived notions of political actors who use historical research to set the stage for their own performances. When this happens, academic history embodies the disruption between thought and action that sophistic historians like Thucydides and Plutarch sought to mend.

Sophistic history flourishes in the world of action, where it engages the forms of popular communication: video, cinema, records, magazines and sometimes books. It is in the meeting halls and courts and commercial centers where the invention of the past serves an immediate purpose. That is why the invention of the past is so influential in determining who we are as a people and as a culture. "Making history" is part and parcel of the larger search for a national self. It is conducted by the mythifiers of our past, not only the popular historians whose appeal rests as much with their literary skills as it does with their research, but also our politicians and pundits and poets of public relations. For these are the true historians of our time. While they self-consciously construct their pleasing portraits of our common heritage, they dabble unknowingly and capriciously with the archaic forces buried deep in the collective subconscious. The division between myth and fact is as indistinct for us as it was for the cultivated minds of ancient Greece. Indeed, "factness" itself is a realm for dispute in a world grown accustomed to novelty, change, and relativity.

Sophistic history, originally a democratic invention, can also be made to serve the totalitarian mind. The 20th century is filled with examples. Stalin used cinematic mass communication to recast his role in the Russian Revolution and to buttress a personal cult of hero worship. In the movies, he plays a major part in the crucial events of 1917 whereas in fact he was not as close either to Lenin or to the front lines as his celluloid projection makes it seem. Hitler, too, understood the power of sophisticated "seeming to be." Nazi film makers have left a legacy which our own political media masters replicate: the staged scene, the multitude of flags and symbols and icons of power, the adoring crowd photographed with uplifted hopeful faces, the martial music, the invocation to a heroic past, the associations with an inevitable future, the flattering camera angles and lighting intended to apotheosize the leader. All sophisticated political leaders practice a form of hagiography in which the facts of a life are reinvented to suit the pretensions of the present. Each becomes a legend in his own time. Personal mythology overwhelms the facts of the case. Recent events present even more vivid instances of the ersatz manufacturing of history. Following the Tianamen Massacre in China, the manipulation of the immediate past took place before the eyes of the world, on the nightly newscasts beamed out of Beijing by the communist authorities. Cause and effect were reversed, careful editing of the television images transformed the aggressors into victims, and news announcers reiterated time and again the Party's basic line. Soldiers were used to suppress hooliganism and terrorism. Reactionary forces were subdued. The country was saved. Reports of the slaughter were greatly exaggerated. Everything has returned to normal.

These, however, are the grossest examples of the uses of history in a sophisticated age. They disclose, among other things, the danger that exists when the mind turns history into poetry without regard to the character of the representation. They also demonstrate on a grand scale a central fact of our time. The poetic of history plays a central role in everyday life. Pretense and imitation are the basic skills of personal and political survival. Sophistic present-mindedness demands control of the past. The confidence and belief that emanate from the contingent verisimilitude depend on an invented chronology to explain how things came to be as they are. We all participate in the destruction of certainty. In a sophisticated age, it works to individual advantage to do away with concrete realities. The more fluid and flexible the present, the greater the opportunity for advancement, personal security, financial success, and ethical ambiguity. Self-doubt and self-confidence work together and ignorance often surpasses knowledge as a warrant for action. The social, political, and commercial fabric of the modern world is held together by our capacity to invent the past. Like Thucydides we are always explaining how matters came to be as they are. Like Plutarch, we are always seeking the grounds that justify our behavior amid ever-present change. The difference between our times and theirs is one of scale and complexity. Our penchant for historicizing penetrates every aspect of community. A few examples are sufficient to indicate the mundane power of sophistic history in our strange times.

Corporations reinterpret their own histories every year when they issue an annual report that explains recent management decisions in terms of uncontrollable precedents, long-term conditions, wise decisions by present owners or unwise actions by former executives. The annual report is a rhetorical art form of the most advanced kind. It aims to put the best light on recent financial performance by inventing a plausible history to be read in the context of immediate circumstances. It is only when a doubting shareholder looks beyond the self-contained and self-validating arguments of the narrative to the financial assessment, or reviews the past decade's annual reports in succession, or relies on some other external form of evidence, that corporate history making comes under fire. Then, one contingent verisimilitude is substituted for another, the doubter's for the company's, and the basis for argument shifts to yet another set of interpretations and assertions. Arguments about the past disguise questions about the present and doubts about the future. Sophistic history is an art of perspective and persuasion.

Politicians make history when they explain present legislation in the context of previous bills and statutes, or when they assert the "true" meaning of prior legislative intent. Truth is a negotiable commodity in politics. Ambiguity is the coin of the realm. Politics, the art of the possible, is formed and informed by rhetoric, the art of the probable. Thucydides' great invention of a sophisticated political history provides us with the macrocosmic science through which politics can be analyzed in detail. It sets up a dialectic between past and present that produces interpretations, preparations and corrections of political assumptions and public policy. For better or worse, Thucydides causes us to regard politics as a central concern of everyday life and a legitimate subject for study. Politics has become an art of public performance dominated by the power of images and emotions. Words have lost their meaning except in the immediate context of application. Change is inevitable and truth is relative. The present age of sophistication shares with that of Thucydides' the sense that everything has changed except the inclination of human beings to misrepresent themselves. The basis of political history itself has been altered by events in the world that defy classification in the old categories or expression in the old terms. The modern politician, like his ancient Greek counterpart, must be a master of the contingent verisimilitude. The past is only a form of "seeming to be," constructed willy-nilly to justify the present and to prejudice the future. Sophistic history is an art of appearance and impressions.

Lawyers invent the past by discovering in the records of previous trials and court rulings the relevant precedents to support present arguments and control potential verdicts. The hallmark of life in the *polis* was the growth of codified law and the reliance on public debate to determine the validity of traditional ways of behaving. The sophists earned their livelihood first in the courts, then in the public meeting places, and finally in the private homes of the wealthy, by demonstrating the power of the new way of arguing both sides of a question. The Greeks conceived of law as a force that spoke to every man directly. The sophists of antiquity promised to empower any person who could pay their fees to hear what the laws had to say and to turn them to personal advantage. Now, the laws speak generally to all people, and rarely with a clear voice. Lawyers are our interpreters of what is really being said. As such, they need to construct a past for law in general and for all laws in their particularity. The paradox, of course, is that while we may conceive of ours as a nation of laws, we are actually a nation of law-givers. Sophistic history is an art of advantage and opportunity.

In a sophisticated age, every person becomes a historian of his own successes and failures. Every time we attempt to explain why we think or believe or act as we do, we use our historical sense to justify our actions, to our selves and to others. The past is an afterthought, not an antecedent, to the present. It supports interpretations of how we came to be as we are in every realm of living that is controlled by the dialogue between thought and action. Sophistic history is egocentric. It radiates from the desire of the individual mind to institute order, coherence and control over the apparent ambiguity and chaos of an ever-changing world. On a daily basis, each one of us practices a small part of Thucydides' great art. We seek the patterns of change that account for the present state of affairs and activate the potentiality of the future. *The History of the Peloponnesian War* is much more than a cultural artifact that should be studied for information about the distant, remote past. Nor is it simply an early form of some academic discipline we call "history." Rather, Thucydides' work is a key archaeological instrument for excavating the many layers of the sophisticated mind. He provides the basis for reconstructing the story of civilization by taking as a starting point the neglected impulses of sophistic epistemology and the misconceived purposes of rhetoric. Such a course would do much to explain the current conditions of life in our own sophisticated world. Sophistic history always provides the background for understanding the emergence of the self within the greater precincts of nation and culture.

The present also resembles Plutarch's age, when rhetorical self-consciousness determined the relationship between individual being and social character. Plutarch sought to invent the models of thought, expression and action that could guide the emergence of Graeco-Roman culture. He was concerned, that is, with the formation of character at a time when ethical conduct, traditional religion and clear national identity were passing away. His *Parallel Lives* documents the search after self in the most abstract sense, as a collection of virtues culled from the examples of the past. Like Thucydides, he also sought the essential foundations of individual being in the manifestations of social character.

Our age is premised on a conception of history that combines aspects of Thucydides and Plutarch. It draws on the rhetorical aesthetic principles of our sophisticated age. History constitutes a new kind of imaginative poetry, though it also employs the most advanced methods of analysis, interpretation and judgment. It is formed and propagated by the tools and techniques of modern mass communication, though it elevates the level of popular discourse about things past and present. History regards probability, opportunism and relativity as conditions of life, though it also seeks the universal principles which shape the character of all human beings. It is concerned with the emergence of an international sophistic culture that is powered by high technology, democratic politics, market economics and sophistic rhetoric. But ultimately sophisticated history supports the search by each individual mind for self-consciousness and self-knowledge in a world where knowledge is fleeting, the past is a figment of the imagination, and the present is merely a precarious, cacophonous, ephemeral moment in time. Sophisticated history penetrates to the core of the relationship between individual being and social character. It investigates and interprets both the culture within which it arises and the people who employ its techniques and engage its forms of thought, expression, and action. It is in the here-and-now that the true power of sophistic thought makes itself known. The history of the present is being written everyday in the realms of thought and action—politics, education and ethics—where individuals pursue their interests in the context of larger social needs. The tensions that inevitably arise between self-interest and the common good are the real sources of our art, our selves and our sophisticated culture.

What Plutarch says about historical research also applies to us as we invent a past for our sophisticated present and future: "I have traversed those periods of time which are accessible to probable reasoning and which afford the basis for a history dealing with facts. What lies beyond is full of marvels and unreality, a land of poets and fabulists, of doubt and obscurity."

The Purpose of History in a Sophisticated Age

CHAPTER THREE

Creating the Present:
The Power of
Sophisticated Politics

Practical politics consists in ignoring facts.
—Henry Adams

B Y THEIR VERY EXISTENCE, politics and rhetoric seem to con-
firm the powerful notion that people are incapable of
dealing directly, truthfully, honestly with one another. To
the person who wants to believe that life can be lived on the
surface, they reek of cynicism and a too-willing acceptance of
the frailty of humankind. The idealist in us believes that our
world would be better if only we could rid ourselves of politics
and rhetoric, if only people could speak their minds without
pretense and could pursue their interests without guile.

History, and the facts of life, argue otherwise. In sophisticated society, where image, appearance and public perception
are fundamental realities, politics and rhetoric are the primary
mechanisms for the realization of both individual being and
social character. They control not only what others think of us
but also what we think of ourselves and our world. It is mislead-
ing and self-deluding to wish that things could be otherwise.
For the idealist who despises politics as a profession engages in
political behavior every day, on the job, at home, among friends
and wherever personal desires and goals must be fulfilled in a

social context. The purist who resents another person's "rhetoric" employs a rhetorical talent of his own in the defense of self-satisfying opinions and the pursuit of self-serving interests.

Politics is the art of the possible. It operates in the realm of communal thought and action where each one of us lives a life connected to others. It has always been closely linked with rhetoric, the art of the probable, since the fulfillment of possibilities requires a sure sense of what other people are willing to do in any particular circumstance to accomplish their ends. Possibility and probability are the conditions of everyday life in a world where personal ambition must constantly adjust to social and psychological constraints and influences. This view is neither as novel nor as accommodating as it seems.

Politics and rhetoric, as descriptive terms as well as active arts, are Greek inventions from the fifth century B.C. They deal with the manifestations of "seeming to be" that bind the abstract realm of talk to the concrete world of concerted action. They exist in reflexive relationship to one another. Political processes and rhetorical techniques evolved hand-in-hand in the wild intellectual ferment of classical Greek society. Through the ministry of Gorgias, Protagoras and other sophistic thinkers, the dawning awareness of personal power and communal sovereignty were honed into something approaching a theory of society. It took shape in the invented histories celebrating the power of individuals to decide their own fate in collaboration with others of like mind. The sophistic view of society granted to the many the authority that had previously rested in the hands of the few. Probability, opportunity and relativity became the keystones of a politics that transformed traditional power arrangements and social expectations into new and powerful expressions of communal reality. The political novelties of the Greeks—written laws, constitutionally prescribed duties and authorities, defined institutions of government—were all premised on a participatory process of collective decision-making grounded in public discussion and debate.

The world of the Greek city-state was at once ordered and expanded by politics and rhetoric. Greek society and ultimately Western Culture acquired powerful ideas from the early sophists, especially the notion that community is something organic, dynamic, mutable. Sophistic rhetoric joins a novel psychology of personal being to a persuasive method for the expression of personal ambition in the public sphere. Sophistic politics links a novel theory of society to a participatory process for the execution of the collective will. Together, politics and rhetoric instill a kind of self-awareness that operates simultaneously and dialectically at two levels, within the society at large and within the mind of individual citizens.

We have grown accustomed to the linkage between public power, public performance and public participation in politics. These sophistic notions are of historic interest not simply because they underwrote the fledgling democracies of the Greek city-states. They are also relevant to us because they support the fundamental processes and principles that animate the emergence of modern democracies around the world. The free flow of ideas between individuals destroys the regimen of a community narrowly anchored in the use of force. It parallels in many ways the evolution of democracy that Thucydides traces in the opening chapters of *The Peloponnesian War,* where he describes the evolutionary pattern that societies ever since have followed as they move from the rule of one or a few to the rule of the many. The process is by no means simple. It involves forces that infiltrate every aspect of communal living, from religion and morality to economics and law. Modest, closed communities evolve into complex, open trading societies. Foreign influences and customs penetrate the native culture along with imported goods, commodities and the borrowed techniques of management and production. Cultural self-awareness is spurred by comparison with alien and forbidden ideas about what constitutes the good life. A complicated intellectual, moral and pragmatic cross-fertilization takes place. Old values are supplanted by new ones and traditional ways of conducting the public's business are replaced by new systems of commerce, government, education and justice.

As Thucydides discovered, experimentation is the hallmark of progress, and change is its measurement. These principles implicitly order the conduct of life everyday on a planet organized around technological innovation and mass communication. The difference between us and the Greeks inheres in the speed with which change occurs. Ideas in ancient Greece travelled no faster than a man on foot, on horseback, or aboard a ship at sea. Today, they circle the globe at the speed of light.

Until the appearance of the sophists, Greek society moved in accordance with deeper currents of social organization and personal understanding. It was based firmly on notions about the cosmos and man's position in it that had held true for over a millennium. An ancient Greek could admit that the natural world was full of surprises, and wonder about the hidden causes of physical change around him. But his social world was based on certainties about power and position that drew their strength from time-honored distinctions between men. The sophists upended these notions. Before they arrived on the scene, power was husbanded within a bewildering web of familial, tribal, and social associations. Their radical program, however, made power available to anyone who could seize and hold it. After them, it was the capacity of the mind to create power itself that determined the potency of the individual within the social realm.

Power for the sophist flows *from minds in agreement*. It exists from moment-to-moment, as the artificial, temporary product of discussion and consent. To be sure, it is possible to gain assent at the point of a sword or from the barrel of a gun or even through lying. But the resort to coercion through superior strength or intellectual dishonesty breaks the psychological bond that rhetoric establishes between the persuader and the persuaded. It gives lie to the confidence in our own unique powers to produce *conviction* as well as action. The distinction is everywhere relevant in Thucydides. He often juxtaposes reports of debates (invented and otherwise) with the actions that resulted from them in order to detail the circumstances within which persuasion becomes coercion and argument evolves into war. He continually demonstrates that the transformation of political discussion into military conflict is an almost accidental process that passes unnoticed by the participants. They cannot maintain a clear perception of the difference between facts and fictions, rumors and realities.

In a civilization controlled by law and debate, which the sophists envisioned to be the highest attainment of human evolution, rhetoric and politics come to express the duality of human nature. On one hand, they empower the individual to pursue his interests against those of his fellows. They mark an inviolable distance between human beings and establish each of us as sovereign in our person. On the other hand, they compel us to act in unison, and provide the mechanisms for deciding which causes and which effects of human action are to be the sole source of what we know at any given time about any particular issue. Politics and rhetoric are primarily concerned with securing, exercising, preserving and transmitting power. In sophisticated society, power flows from the ability to influence others through pretense, skillful representation and the fabrication of influential contingent verisimilitudes.

Politics is dedicated to the creation of a useful, pervasive present. Past and future are plastic constructions projected from the evidence of the "now." They possess no objective reality. They are functions of necessity and speculation, of yearning and desire. In the sophisticated age, politics has but one purpose: to fashion a serviceable reality that temporarily unites different people and interests in common action.

That is why modern scholars—and ancient thinkers such as Thucydides, Plato and Aristotle—take pains to describe politics as a verbal system or argumentative method or social operation or institutional process that is known by its products and ends. They seek to anchor it, that is, in some substitute reality such as logic or art or science or philosophy. From these different bases, they can then analyze the operations of politics and discover, at least, that it is in some way connected to the phenomenon of language and the power of speech. It acquires both a form and a psychology. Politics expresses the authority of the group in words and images that embody the underlying values, biases, fears, desires, predispositions and preferences of synthetic communities. It is essentially emotional. It plays on the rudimentary passions, although at every turn we pretend to rationalize it through law and government; to fix it, that is, to a firm foundation of precedent and predictability. Sophisticated politics is nominally democratic since it draws its strength from the participation in its verisimilitudes of some constitutionally defined majority. It envisions a sovereignty based on numbers, not on nature. Yet sophisticated political power requires the conscious manipulation of symbols and signs, images and words, people and events that can be performed only by a class of specialists who are schooled in the tools and techniques of rhetoric—our politicians, pollsters, pundits and the poets of public relations. Outwardly egalitarian, it actually promotes the exploitation of the naive by the urbane. It is an oligarchy of merit masking as a democracy of opportunity. Consequently, sophisticated political power is paradoxical. It traffics in promises and potentialities, since its pervasive present-mindedness always has an eye on some future purpose. It shuns stability, predictability and certainty since these are the hallmarks of the unsophisticated mind. It flourishes amid ambiguity, variation, and expedience. It presumes that there are no large solutions for the problems of community. All truths are temporary and relative. Process is more important than product. Information is power. Words are tools. Images are real. Change is inevitable.

Contradictory political organizations of all kinds, from the democratic to the totalitarian, have been built upon the commonplaces of sophistic thought, on its organizational innovations and its argumentative techniques. Despite marked differences in ideology, sovereignty, or authority that distinguish different forms of social control, the institutional expressions of sophisticated politics share one overriding similarity. They constitute the basis for communal judgment and action amid the flux and flow of an ever-changing, humanly determined history. Indeed, in the sophisticated age, politics comprises reality itself.

Despite their relevance to the political order of our times, the sophists of ancient Greece are largely unknown to us. Their writings have long been lost. If we hear of them at all it is usually in the commentaries of others who had reasons aplenty for spurning the sophistic agenda. The dynamic of the sophistic mind is imbedded paradoxically in the reaction of Plato (428–347 B.C.) to the sophistic epistemology and in the accommodation of Aristotle (384–322 B.C.) to sophistic techniques of argument and government. With respect to politics, Plato and Aristotle represent two positions on sophistic thought. A third position is embodied in the example of Demosthenes (384–322 B.C.), the Athenian orator who unsuccessfully sought to stem the tide of Macedonian imperialism in the fourth century B.C. by preserving the unique culture of the independent Greek city-state. Indeed, all three anchored their conceptions of politics in the viability of the *polis*. It represented for them the highest, most refined, most rational form of communal living. Anything smaller would be powerless to control its own fate; anything larger, unwieldy and slow to act. For us, the term *polis* penetrates and enlivens the vocabulary of community we employ every day, when we talk of politicians and the politics they practice, the policies they make and the polities they lead.

Plato, Aristotle and Demosthenes present a complex continuum of thought and action from which politics receives its characteristic reifications in the sophisticated world. Each expresses essential elements of self-government in its most particular senses—as a concept of individual being as well as social responsibility—that exert a powerful influence over our own response to the ambiguities of life in society. The broader philosophic tensions between the positions they represent find expression not only in contemporary politics but also in education, ethics and aesthetics. For these arenas of thought and action are closely related to politics. Consequently, the Platonist, Aristotelian and sophistic positions that can be isolated in the ancient world provide distinctions by which we can know our own time, our own sophistication and our own selves.

These three ancient minds expressed themselves in idiosyncratic forms. Plato developed the dialogue as the ideal vehicle for his analysis of the perfect state. Aristotle composed lectures and treatises that analyzed forms of government in existing imperfect states and compared their limitations and advantages. Demosthenes, however, constructed pragmatic arguments and speeches, not philosophic dialogues or educational treatises. His orations reflected the realities of power and exemplified the pervasive penetration of politics into every facet of life in a single *polis*, Athens. The three also treated language differently. For Plato, words are the veil of unreality that obscures our understanding of truth and promotes the flawed politics of emotion. For Aristotle, language merely reflects in one degree of accuracy or another the substantial, underlying relationship between ideas and things, thoughts and actions, that in their totality make up the reasonable world. For Demosthenes, words are masks to be donned by the craftsman of government, the orator, in the political dramas he constructs for the edification of his fellow citizens. He alone is capable of fashioning the serviceable realities of sophisticated politics by moving men to common action through appeals to emotion, desire and even reason. In their often contradictory ways, Plato and Aristotle attacked sophistic thinking across a broad front, from its reliance on moral relativity to its promotion of democratic ideals and institutions. In turn, they each constructed often opposed visions of reality in order to answer the sophists' twofold claim to know the world and to teach how that knowledge could be used for personal gain.

If Thucydides invented history to account for the profound social and political sophistication of Greece, Plato and Aristotle can be said to have invented the formal study of politics and rhetoric to rationalize Greek culture. They laid the intellectual groundwork for the study of sophistication in all its manifestations—as history, language, power, knowledge, art and action. Plato was born at the outset of Thucydides' war and matured in the generation immediately following the most prominent sophists, Gorgias, Hippias and Protagoras. His 80 years encompassed the giddy heights and profound depths of Athenian culture. His student Aristotle inherited a world conditioned by the influence of sophistic ideas and Plato's reaction to them. It was a far more cynical place than the Athens of Plato's dialogues. Greece had lost her innocence. She had become sophisticated. And Aristotle played various roles in the regime of sophistic thought, first as Plato's student then as tutor to Alexander and finally as founder of a school of thought that trod a middle course between Plato's academic idealism and sophistic political pragmatism. In different ways and to different ends, both grappled with an evolving circumstance that required new forms of thought and expression. Eventually, Plato and Aristotle turned their characteristic responses to sophistic thought into arts of one kind or another.

Plato poured his analysis into dialogues where his characters argued over the moral, political and social issues of the day. His dialogues are at once a dramatic rendering of the life of reason and a picture of a state of mind. They are documents relevant to a society in which current intellectual interests have been stimulated and motivated by new and revolutionary forces. Plato's Athens exists as both a moment in time and as a psychological reality that impinged on the development of individual being as well as social character. She fostered reformers and doers, liberals and conservatives, pragmatists and idealists.

Athenian innovation and daring became the envy of Greece. In the eyes of more traditional societies such as arch rival Sparta, Athens posed the greatest threat not only to time-honored customs and beliefs but also to proven arrangements in the structure of power and authority. Athenian politics bounced along an uneven path, swerving first toward the anarchy of the mob and then toward the absolutism of tyrants and oligarchs, from the rule of the many to the rule of the few or the one. The unpredictability of her democratic institutions, the internecine rivalry of her factions, and the mercantile aspirations of her burgeoning population combined to make Athens the engine that drove sophisticated politics in the Hellenic world. In the decade before Plato's birth she emerged as the preeminent force in panhellenic affairs. Politics and rhetoric united to produce a paradoxical Athenian ethos perhaps best embodied in the character of her most famous citizen, Pericles. His influence was so pervasive and persistent that the city was a democracy in name only, as Thucydides pointed out. She prospered under the rule of one man who rose to power by speaking on behalf of the masses.

Thucydides argues that the downfall of Athens became inevitable once the sure hand of Pericles passed from the tiller of state. Such was the paradoxical power of Athen's foremost citizen. He attracted admirers and enemies alike. He was born into the upper reaches of society but built his constituency among its lower classes. He paid homage to the city's traditions and gods and at the same time set about reshaping her social hierarchy through the liberalization of politics. More to the point, he attracted a great number of sophists to Athens, gave them beds and fed them meals in his own home and, by his association with them, legitimized their message and method. He also entertained a courtesan of remarkable learning and skill, Aspasia, who would be charged during Pericles' rare moments of political weakness with crimes against the city's honor as well as its religious laws. He embarked on an ambitious foreign policy that sought to secure the city's control over the Aegean Sea in order to safeguard the trade routes with its Black Sea granaries. He mixed in one person, that is, all the contradictory and competing qualities of the Athenians themselves. Thucydides makes him the personification of the Athenian character. History has forever linked him with the Golden Age of Greece.

The ironic nature of Periclean rule and of Athens itself motivated Plato to explore the fundamental questions of life in community that inevitably surfaced amid the obvious contradictions between what Athenians thought, what they said and what they did. His great genius is to illuminate the paradoxes of everyday life by making the characters of his dialogues voice competing concepts of reality, knowledge, virtue and truth. He addresses at the most essential level the same contrary characteristics that Thucydides discerned in the flow of Athenian history. Like Thucydides, Plato captures the spirit of the times in the speech, thoughts, inventions, actions and personalities of human beings who argue as if life itself depended on the outcome. The reader is often struck by the intellectual energy of the participants in Plato's dialogues. To be sure, he sets up his characters as straw men with straw arguments to be batted down by an overpowering Socrates using an irresistible dialectical logic. But beneath the interplay of the topical disputes there lurks a portrait of the place and the times that transcends immediate circumstances or concerns. Athens is populated by people who are mindfully constructing a community from the ground up. Mindful, too, are they of their heritage, the historic foundation of their city and its unique role in the evolution of Greece. The sophists have taught them how to harness an artificially interpreted past in the service of a powerfully asserted, pervasive and, to Plato, ultimately catastrophic present.

The sophistic confidence in the power of human imagination finds in Plato an inverted and often troubling expression. The same talents that have liberated the mind of the common man turn out to be the root causes for the downfall of a city and a civilization. Pericles' great political reforms, such as the payment of jurors and the expansion of the franchise, eventually rebound against the city after his death. Both Thucydides and Plato lay the blame on Cleon, the wealthy tanner who succeeded Pericles in the midst of the Peloponnesian War but could never match his predecessor's ability to bring Athens' warring factions together. In their eyes, Cleon is the prime example of sophistic power gone wrong, a man who usurped the natural order of things and brought Athens to disaster.

It is fashionable to chalk up Plato's characterizations, complaints and opinions about democratic rule to the disaffections of an oligarch. He was high born and thus disturbed by the demeaning transformations in power that Pericles' political reforms inevitably brought to Athens. Like Thucydides, he too had personal grounds for holding a grudge against the rule of the many. Plato's reaction to sophistic thought was clearly conditioned in part by his dismay over the fate of Socrates. For him, the distemper of the paid Athenian jurors who tried and condemned Socrates was grounded in assumptions and embodied in arguments that smacked of sophistic relativism. The charges themselves—that Socrates was guilty of impiety, of teaching strange doctrines and of corrupting the city's youth—were sophistically employed by unscrupulous partisans to paint Socrates a sophist, despite his lifelong rejection of sophistry and his well known suspicions of rhetoric. Ever since, Socrates has been adjudged a partisan of the aristocrats, a closet oligarch who supported the overthrow of Athenian democracy and abetted the subsequent oligarchic terrors, purges and exiles. For Plato, the sin against Socrates was rooted in far deeper undercurrents of Athenian life. His mentor was condemned amid the confusion that followed Athens' defeat in the Peloponnesian War, when shifting alliances transformed normally stable relationships between sectors of society into a cauldron of recrimination and betrayal. The Athenians forgot Socrates lifelong service to her, in Plato's eyes, in order to satisfy an immediate pang for revenge.

All of this serves as background to understanding Plato's greatest work, the *Republic*. This dialogue portrays at great length his reaction to the influence of sophistic thought in Athens. Actually, we do an injustice to translate Plato's title *Politeia* as "republic." The Latin *res publica* captures only a part of the spirit of the work. The dialogue certainly deals with public affairs in the broadest sense, such as the relationship between parts of the state or government or constitution of the *polis*.

But the utopian state described in the *Politeia* has very little to do with the form of government we would recognize as republican, either in its construction, operation or purpose. If Plato's ideal state is a republic at all, it is a republic of ideas and superior minds. Sovereignty and power are based on expertise, knowledge, intellectual capability and the mastery of dialectic. The world portrayed in the *Politeia* is utopian to the extent it is ordered by the imperatives of reason. Indeed, the dialogue is concerned ultimately with justice, of the well-ordered life expressed by the example of the well-ordered city. As an examination of the just rendering of life, the *Politeia* is consumed with the paradoxes surrounding the desire for community. It is a dialogue on "cityness" that begins with the superficial, artificial problems of government and ends up exploring the profound difficulties of self-knowledge and self-control in a world marked by desire, appetite, lust and greed. It portrays at many levels the unceasing dialogue between individual being and social character that Plato saw working itself out in the years of his maturation, a period that reaches its climax with the death of Socrates.

Plato's concern for justice and his treatment in the *Politeia* of both the well-ordered state and the well-ordered soul entail the central question of all his earlier dialogues. What is the good life? The question, while simple to state, is difficult to answer. It requires, among other things, an understanding of human nature, of the emotions and motives that constitute the inventive mind at work in the world. It also requires an understanding of goodness, not as it is expressed in many dissimilar deeds or examples but as a thing in itself. And these two requirements entail a third. True understanding flows from the right kind of education. Consequently, Plato constructs the *Politeia* around the central questions of life and learning. What do we know? How do we know that we know? How do we tell what we know?

The dialogue on the ideal state becomes a dialogue on the state of man in community. After all, the good life can only be examined in its communal aspect. Doctrines appearing elsewhere in Plato are here concentrated around the wide-ranging search for the good life. Virtue is knowledge and the soul is immortal. Poetry and poets are immoral since they distract us with fictions and teach us to admire products of the human imagination that misrepresent reality and so mislead the impressionable mind. The rule of the many is absurd and dangerous, for democracy pays no heed to merit or natural qualifications for office. Politics is no art since it has no purpose other than control and seeks, instead, to play on the baser emotions of human beings.

The city Plato describes in the *Politeia* banishes not only poets but also sophists. For his examination of the three questions of knowledge that motivated the sophistic epistemology results in a quite different sense of reality. What a sophist would regard as airy abstractions Plato portrays as the only real things. How else, he asks time and again, can we know anything if not through its relation to some universal, pervasive, inspiring, ideal form? The virtues of the sophistic world—change, appearance, timeliness, opportunism, probability, relativity—are in the *Politeia* symptoms of human error, misunderstanding, fallibility and failure. For Plato, the politicians are the undertakers of Hellenic freedom. The more they act on behalf of the people of Athens, the faster the city devolves into chaos and corruption. The sophistic confidence in the human imagination is met with Platonic doubt in the capacity of the mind to know anything, much less to act reasonably on that at best partial knowledge.

The perfect state, however, is led by philosopher-kings who attain their office after long years of education and service. Dialectic, not rhetoric, is the true art of government. Throughout the *Politeia*, Plato describes dialectic as engaged in a war over the soul. At one level, it is fought in terms of right government and justice, of the right rule of those who know over those who are entrapped by ignorance. At another level, the war over the soul is waged in terms of righteous action by the individual. The supreme virtues of self-knowledge and self-control are cultivated through the exercise of dialectical self-examination. Plato's ideal state thus stands in direct opposition to the sophist's *realpolitik*, where verbal suasion greased by the appearance of sincerity and the power of the contingent verisimilitude forms the basis for collective judgment and action.

Paradoxically, Plato's own contingent verisimilitude, the *Politeia*, argues against the veracity of poetic or political fictions. It lays out the grand mechanisms of power that can shape the characters of human beings in their daily lives. No wonder that with the passing of time, the Platonic school of philosophy withdrew from political life. It came to be viewed with suspicion by the sophisticated politicians who assumed power after Athens' defeat in the Peloponnesian War. The influence of Socrates and Plato on the city's young could only be regarded with alarm by those who sought to base the revival of power in the common expressions of popular will. Plato's Academy was perhaps the first monastic response to the decline of a civilization and after the *Politeia* was completed it became increasingly more concerned with mathematics and abstract learning. Plato's reaction to the sophisticated world was to withdraw into the deep recesses of pure thought.

Aristotle found much to disagree with in both the form and content of his teacher's writings. He lived in a world of natural phenomenon and it is no accident that he is credited with the development of the scientific method. Aristotle was an observer as much as a thinker. His appreciation for the multiplicity and variety of nature led him toward a logic of differentiation and classification as opposed to Plato, who labored to find the essential unity behind apparent diversity. But Aristotle held no brief with Plato's solution, the Theory of Forms. It was for him false on the face of it, implying an infinite regression of forms behind forms with no possibility of a substantial reality that could be known, much less grappled with, by means of the senses. Rather, Aristotle sought to see things as they were, in terms of their parts and processes and ends. Similarity and difference are the organizing principles of his philosophy. If Plato's cosmos shimmers with a sense of the divine and the eternal, Aristotle's vibrates with mutability and the commonplace.

Then, too, Aristotle's formative years were markedly different from Plato's. He was born into a world where Periclean Athens was only a vague memory and Socrates, a literary inspiration. The Peloponnesian War changed the Greek political landscape forever, setting in motion a series of events that would make possible the rise of Macedonia and, more important, the fall of the *polis* as a vital unit of self-government. As Plato's student, Aristotle would study the philosophic themes explored by the early sophists Gorgias, Protagoras and Hippias. Their works as well as his master's treatment of them were available to him. As a worldly teacher in the court of the Macedonian king he could listen to the debates about policies propounded in the studied eloquence of Aeschines and Demosthenes, exemplar orators of a newer sophistic age.

It was this unique marriage of idealistic education and pragmatic experience that framed Aristotle's consideration of politics and rhetoric. The two are intimately linked. Human beings are by nature political animals. They seek the comfort and strength of their fellows in community. All communities aim at some good, according to Aristotle, and the highest of these, the political community, "which embraces all the rest," aims at the highest good. The need to commune is the impulse that gives rise to politics and the mechanism for the political realization of community is the gift of speech. Nature makes nothing in vain and the power of speech—not mere vocalization of pleasures and pains, but coherent, intentional utterance—helps us articulate the major issues of life in community: action and inaction, expediency and inexpediency, justice and injustice. Aristotle treats politics and rhetoric as discrete yet interrelated arts, each with its own subject matter, method and end. Thoroughly human arts though they are, they can be approached with the same care that Aristotle employs in the study of natural phenomena although they defy the same degree of exactitude.

Politics and rhetoric deal with the vagaries of human thought and action. They constitute the realm of uncertainty that is described by a readily observable fact: people often say things they do not mean, mean things they do not say, and act in ways contrary to either their statements or their thoughts. Knowledge of the disjunction between what we mean, what we say and what we do has a pragmatic value. It can serve as the basis for a practical political science that is useful both for describing existing forms of government and for establishing successful states based on real models.

Politics derives from two sources. First, it arises from the common characteristics of polity, the formal notion of "community," that can be discovered from close analysis of the operations of different states. This analysis identifies the basic relationships between the individual and the community, law and justice, power and authority, that in their peculiar mixture cast a system as predominantly democratic, monarchic, oligarchic or tyrannical. Second, political science also investigates the nature of the ideal *polis* by looking to the best states of history and the best states imagined by theorists like Plato. The exercise of isolating and describing the ideal state carries a distinctly pragmatic purpose, since any discussion of politics aims ultimately to discover the nature of the communal good and how best to attain it. Inquiring after the ideal life can lead us to an appreciation of what is both good and useful in mundane affairs. The pursuit of the ideal is not a sophistic exercise, intended to dazzle or impress. Rather, the inquiry is undertaken simply because "all the constitutions with which we are acquainted," Aristotle writes, "are faulty." Although politics is ultimately a practical art for Aristotle, it is not simply reducible to a set of rules or procedures. Unlike the utopian *Politeia*, Aristotle's *Politics* is descriptive rather than prescriptive. It sets out to survey, classify, analyze and compare all types of political systems, real and imagined.

Moreover, Aristotle carefully establishes the relationship between the arts of politics and rhetoric in a manner that clearly distinguishes his analysis of community from Plato's, on the one hand, and the sophists', on the other. Plato sought the basis of community in its abstract form. His *Politeia* is not a practical treatise on government, descriptive of the parts and functions of the state. It is a reverie of sorts, a contemplation on the theme of justice as it can be bodied forth in the construction of the ideal society. Plato need not bother with urban planning of the kind with which we are familiar. His city is populated by people who know their place, guarded by incorruptible police and led by philosophers who understand the intricacies of dialectical logic. It is a world where politics and rhetoric are not only unnecessary, they are absolutely evil. Only dialectic guarantees the smooth, efficient, rational operation of utopia.

If Plato can be accused of ignoring politics and rhetoric in his discussion of the ideal state, the sophists can be said to have demeaned both arts by their practice in the very real states of the Hellenic world. They erred in thinking that judicial pleadings are the sole realm of rhetoric and that appeals to the emotions are its primary means of persuasion. It is, in Aristotle's eyes, a twofold error. Mere sophistry ignores the noble role of political oratory in the daily life of the *polis* by focusing exclusively on the relations of private individuals. Since the practicing sophist either spoke in court on behalf of a client or, more commonly, penned the written appeals that were read by the client himself, he generally argues about matters of no great consequence to the state. Moreover, he is automatically removed from a personal stake in the issue, other than the winning of his fee. And, more grievous still, the sophistic conception of rhetoric narrows the art to its non-essential aspect, emotional appeal, at the expense of means of persuasion based in demonstrative proof. For Aristotle, however, rhetoric is a specie of both politics and ethics. It is no mere set of techniques for arousing pity or anger or fear in a judge. Rather, it a "universal" art without a specific subject matter. But as the "faculty of observing in any given case the available means of persuasion," rhetoric is useful for arguing about matters special to all other arts and sciences. Consequently, its function is not simply to persuade but to discover the means of "coming as near such success" as the circumstances permit.

The peculiar nature of rhetoric, as a universal art concerned with discerning the means of persuasion, lends itself to politics, the art of deciding how the means of the state should be disposed. The one deals with the probabilities of human reasoning while the other treats the possibilities for communal action. Or, put another way, rhetoric and politics are engaged in the intricate consolidation of cause and effect. Rhetoric originates in the goals of the orator and plays itself out in the mechanisms, processes and procedures of the state. Moreover, rhetorical speech—with its emphasis on the character of the speaker, the disposition of the audience and the nature of the subject matter—is determined by the specific structures, or constitutions, of different states. Democracy, monarchy, and oligarchy each have their own forms of public address, debate, deliberation and decision-making. Constitutionally, they are at once politically and rhetorically distinct. Rhetoric takes note of classes of listeners, not individual beings. Its subjects, and the premises from which it argues, present alternative possibilities in the sphere of action. And it must adapt itself to an audience of untrained thinkers.

All this and more, Aristotle claims, is neglected by the sophists. They are intent on producing an effect through emotion and tend to limit themselves to treatises on pleading in court. To the extent that the sophist engages the rhetorical faculty of discerning the means of persuasion, he may be called a "rhetorician." But Aristotle is careful to point out that what makes a man a "sophist" is not his faculty, but his moral purpose. As a universal art with no special subject matter, rhetoric is impartial and amoral. It can serve good or bad ends, but its greatest power is to distinguish between the real and the apparent means of persuasion.

Thus, for Aristotle, rhetoric is an instrument that can be employed in the context of politics to discriminate between appearance and reality. Like Plato, he finds the sophistic emphasis on emotion to be detrimental to wise policy-making and the pursuit of the common good. Unlike Plato, however, Aristotle does not banish the sophists from the state. That would be impossible since at any one time or in any circumstance even the best mind can slip into sophistry. Rather, he invents arts of possibility and probability, politics and rhetoric, that help the mind to navigate amid the flux and flow of "seeming to be." Plato, in contrast, is everywhere and at all times concerned with "being" itself. His ideal state seeks to locate the unchanging grounds of human knowledge and to translate them at every point into right action.

Aristotle also treats the nature of "being" but in a separate treatise called *Metaphysics*. His considerations there certainly bear upon his discussions of politics and rhetoric. But he is careful to separate the theoretical concerns of being from the practical concerns of life in a world constantly on the verge of becoming something else. He does not revel in the contingent verisimilitudes of sophistic thought, however. "Seeming to be" is an imperfect state of mind for Aristotle, fraught with danger and deception. As a basis for common action, it is a poor substitute for demonstrated conclusions. We must penetrate the arguments, examples, assertions, claims and apparent proofs individuals concoct in order to secure the assent of their fellows. The arts of politics and rhetoric describe a sort of calculus for assessing intentions and estimating consequences. Calculation of this sort is based, on one hand, in the characteristic organizations of communal life and, on the other, in the characteristic structures of thought and expression by which we communicate. Together, politics and rhetoric frame our consciousness of the world outside our selves. They are the mechanisms that shape the interaction between individual being and social character.

Aristotle and Demosthenes were born in the same year and died months apart. Their lives were entwined with the career of Alexander the Great. They embody, however, different aspects of political sophistication as it played itself out in the cockpit of Greek politics of the fourth century B.C. As the foremost advocate of Athenian independence from Macedonia, Demosthenes challenged the militaristic politics and imperial pretensions of the Macedonian kings, first Philip and then Alexander. He was a pragmatic politician who used the great issues of the day to

secure power for himself within his *polis*. The community of
Athens was a hard reality for Demosthenes. He drew from it the
inspiration for his defense of its independence. He created for it
a sense of the past and a mission for the future that defined
Athenian honor, nobility and righteousness against the broad
background of Hellenic history. For Demosthenes, the *polis* was
politics and politics, the *polis*.

Aristotle, on the other hand, grew to maturity under Macedonian, not Athenian, rule. If Plato can be said to have attempted
to discover the spiritual unity of the *polis* by elaborating an ideal
state based on its structures and organization, Aristotle seems to
have accepted the diminution of the *polis* as the central political
unit of the Hellenic world. For him, it remained an adequate
expression of Greek civilization, to be sure, but he approaches
its study with a cool eye. Unlike Demosthenes, he saw no advantage in perpetuating a sophistic history of Athens. He was
an interloper in the city's culture, drawn to Athens by Plato and
his school. His dispassionate survey of the many different kinds
of constitutions, over 150, reflects the biologist's regard for the
variety of species, not the politician's passion for power and
independence. Indeed, Aristotle seems not to care whether the
polis survives at all. He dreams neither of a spiritually healed
Hellenic culture nor a tightly bound Athenian state.

Demosthenes was peculiarly Athenian and in his person one
can detect the traits attributed to all Athenians by Thucydides in
a speech he puts into the mouths of the Corinthian ambassadors
at Sparta. The Corinthians are attempting to persuade the Spartans that war with Athens is inevitable, and that its roots lie in
the character of their opponents.

> An Athenian is always an innovator, quick to form a resolution
> and quick at carrying it out . . . . Then again, Athenian daring will
> outrun its own resources; they will take risks against their better
> judgment, and still, in the midst of danger, remain confident . . .
> they never hesitate . . . they are always abroad, for they think that
> the farther they will go the more they will get . . . . If they fail in
> some undertaking, they make good the loss immediately by set-
> ting their hopes in some other direction . . . . Their view of a
> holiday is doing what needs doing; they prefer hardship and

activity to peace and quiet. In a word, they are by nature incapable of either living a quiet life themselves or of allowing anyone else to do so. (I.69)

This is Demosthenes: innovative, daring, dynamic, active,
incessant, unrelenting. His was certainly not a quiet life, and his
involvement in Athenian politics guaranteed that others would
not be left in peace either. He was a passionate politician, given
less to study and speculation than to speech-making and argumentation. Unlike the earlier sophists who earned their living
teaching others the power of sophistic techniques, Demosthenes
wrote no handbooks or manuals. He preferred the public ora-
tion to the private performance or the published tract. The
works of his we possess, all speeches made before the assembly
of Athenians, are tied directly to the issues of his day, some
trivial, most momentous, none obscure or abstract. Engaged,
vital, public minded in the broadest sense, he is the epitome of
the sophists who continued to influence politics in Greece for
several centuries. His mind, in fact, was an arena for the issues
of life in community that Plato had examined through the prism
of literary invention and that Aristotle would analyze system-
atically through the methods of special arts. In the span of 100
years, from Gorgias' arrival in Athens around the middle of the
fifth century B.C. to Demosthenes ascendancy in the city's politics in the mid-fourth century, sophistic thought had found its
place in the cities of Greece. Indeed, it *was* the Greek state. The
ornate, extended discussion of the ideal polity in Plato's *Politeia* is in many respects the last great literary reaction against
sophisticated politicians, much as Thucydides' history of the
Peloponnesian War was perhaps the first. Twenty years or so
separate these works. By the birth of Demosthenes and Aristotle,
in 384 B.C., the sophist had become a fixture in the politics of the
Greek city-state.

Unlike either Plato or Aristotle, who are remote and inacces-
sible to most of us, Demosthenes is a political character we
easily recognize in our own day. Born the son of a wealthy
manufacturer of swords and bed frames, he stood to inherit a
business and a small fortune. His father's early death, however,

resulted in the appointment of three executors who were spend-thrifts on their own behalf. When Demosthenes reached the age of maturity, his first act was to sue his guardians to recover the remainder of his inheritance. It was an auspicious beginning for a man destined for the law courts and assembly.

His career as a rhetorician began, as so many others had, as a writer of speeches for litigants. Apparently, he could compose better than he could speak; he had a weak constitution and a defective voice. Like others of his profession, and lawyers ever since, he was adept at arguing all sides of an issue. It is even rumored that in one case he prepared pleas for both parties in a dispute. He practiced, that is, the relative morality that lies at the heart of sophistication. He also subscribed to the belief in self-confidence and the powers of self-improvement that have formed the sophistic pedagogy ever since Gorgias preached his message of opportunism to eager Greek audiences a century earlier. Demosthenes was not one to leave his handicaps unaddressed. There is the story of his practicing orations at the seashore, where he not only had to overcome the roar of the waves but did so while speaking with his mouth full of pebbles. To build the strength of his lungs, he declaimed while he ran up a hill. He would practice for hours, alternating what we would regard as techniques of speech therapy with drills in memorization and presentation. The years of effort paid off, for he became one of the richest lawyers in Athens, combining the best aspects of that profession, ancient or modern. He understood the technicalities of the law, he was convincing in argument, and he was flexible in his morals.

As a speaker, Demosthenes sometimes employed techniques that we would find amusing and perhaps ineffective, given the cultivation of our ears and eyes by the cooler techniques of modern telecommunications. Still, his speeches reflect the tastes of the common Athenian and represent the kind of discourse that led Plato to despise oratory as the poison of the mind. Rhetoric, for Plato, was the art of governing through feelings and passions. And emotions were the province of Demosthenes. He knew how to work his crowd. Plutarch attributes to him the refinement of practiced eloquence as opposed to the extemporaneous talents of the earlier sophistic period. Demosthenes thought the secret of oratory was acting, what the Greeks called *hypokrisis*, and he rehearsed his speeches until every nuance and witticism was honed to perfection. One story has it that he dug himself a cave and lived in it for months, practicing his art in secret. When he retreated to his cave, it is said, he would leave half of his face unshaven to deter himself from returning to society before he was finished with his work. Whatever the truth of the story, it points to the intensity and nervous energy that was remarked of him throughout his life. He was a grandstanding stem-winder, the William Jennings Bryan of his day. When he hit his stride in a speech, he would make use of his whole body, assuming poses and contorting himself to portray different attitudes. The rostrum was his stage and he would whirl round and round, facing first one side of his audience, then the other. For emphasis, he would lay his hand on his forehead and strike a reflective pose. Often he raised his voice to a scream that could be heard, according to some reports, across all of Athens. He was the consummate demagogue.

"Seeming to be" assumed central importance in the politics and rhetoric of Demosthenes. For him, the orator did not simply speak to an assembly of citizens according to the rules of art. He enacted before them the drama of their lives as it was constituted in the challenges they confronted as a community. He mixed interpretations of the past with impressions of the present in order to secure their approval of future policies. The power of political oratory has always resided within its awe inspiring present-mindedness. It appeals to the capacity for pretense and imitation that lies deep in each of us. The orator spins out his contingent verisimilitudes in order to create an overwhelming moment in time, the here-and-now, within which his listeners find a home for their prejudices and fears, hopes and desires, dreams and aspirations. The orator embodies the passion that moves minds to accord and into action.

Throughout antiquity, Demosthenes represented the supreme achievement of a culture based on words and the power of the contingent verisimilitude. He came to personify the orator as the confluence of compelling human and supernatural forces.

More than anything else, the orator's individual eloquence determined the shape of the social conscience of his time and place. In his own time, Demosthenes was regarded with awe, fear and suspicion because, as a sophisticated politician, he tapped into the primeval urges of society. The Greeks understood the terrifying presence of the articulate voice of the orator, heard above all others, bending minds to its point of view, taking hold of the souls of men and leading them where they could not imagine going alone. Plato would seek to discredit the orator and Aristotle to tame him with an ethical art of invention and presentation. Neither would be successful, for an orator like Demosthenes is neither the product of art nor imagination nor even intellect. He springs out of the society itself to become for a moment in time the robust representation of his community's most fundamental being. He becomes the spirit of the place, the living embodiment of all that can be called culture. His sophistication reflects the temper of his time.

Demosthenes eventually lost his long war with the Macedonians. Shortly after Alexander's untimely death, in 322 B.C., Demosthenes helped organize a revolt in Athens. The Macedonians suppressed it ruthlessly and Demosthenes took refuge in a temple sanctuary. Surrounded by his pursuers, he drank a vial of poison and died. Ever since, the fate of Demosthenes has come to represent the fate of anyone who would exercise the charismatic power of eloquence. He is honored only in death, when the silent void left by his absence becomes the most articulate expression of his strength and skill. The same year that brought the deaths of Alexander and Demosthenes also saw the end of Aristotle. He had long been unpopular in Athens. Plato's Academy, under the direction of lesser minds since his death in 347 B.C., as well as the schools of rhetoric led by prominent sophists, regarded him as a rival, a critic and, worse still, an alien intruder. His Macedonian connections never sat well with native Athenians who were in many respects the haughty Parisians of their day. After Alexander's death, a charge of impiety was brought against Aristotle. He fled to Chalcis where he died, some say of a stomach illness, others, by taking poison.

Plato, Aristotle and Demosthenes are for some merely vague and curious names attached to people who lived in a distant past. Yet they brought into focus ideas about the mind and its search for fellowship that still resonate in our own highly sophisticated, technological world. Politics and rhetoric were born in the crucible of ancient Greece. They were given form and content by Plato, who reacted to them, by Aristotle, who sought to base them in an organized scheme of arts, and by Demosthenes, who employed them to gain personal glory and municipal power. In one way or another all three shaped what it means to seek the good life, for each of us individually as well as for ourselves in community. They set the terms, that is, by which we can understand how our world operates amid change, confusion, and instantaneous communication, the commonplaces of our own sophisticated culture.

As it is now practiced, politics is much more than a method of governing, a system of judging or a science of living in community. It is also the primary arena for self-realization. Politics is the vehicle for the projection of individual being into the realms of social character, for the manifestation of individual desire or "self-interest" in the context of communal needs. Whatever its incarnation as personality or character, sophisticated self-realization looks to the forms and organizing structures of polity to communicate rhetorical self-consciousness. So conceived, politics deals with every aspect of life in community, not simply with the mechanisms of election or the conduct of government. It permeates the commercial, educational, judicial, professional and social realms of our society. For these also involve communities of interest, competing groups and collaborative associations of human beings, each of which generates and dispenses a characteristic form of power. Sophisticated society relies on suasion, not force, to accomplish its ends and to enforce its collective will. The power of sophistication is more an enveloping field of energy than a single bolt of lightening. Its charge can be felt everywhere and at anytime, for it resides in the dominating conviction that the human mind is capable of anything once it joins with others. Through communication, it unites communities by grounding them first in expression, then in action. Sophisticated politics thus eventually obliterates the artificial distinctions between public and private interests, individual being and social character, the one and the many. Pervasive present-mindedness often leads to like-mindedness. And politics, power and persuasion play a central role whenever two or more people are engaged in a common enterprise.

In the ancient Greek *polis*, politics was the center of the city and its citizens. A man could aspire to no higher honor than to serve in public life. Individual success was bound up with the successful fulfillment of a city's political destiny. Both the individual and the nurturing *polis* were engaged in an intricate dialogue across time that placed a premium on intellectual inventiveness and the power of words. Public speech assumed a central role in politics for it alone could inform the intangible aspirations of individuals and knit together the framework for their fulfillment in collective action. The ancient sophist promised to teach all comers the secrets of self-expression that were key to rising in the public sphere, to becoming a leader of men and a shaper of the future. Self-expression, in turn, was linked to self-confidence. In a world conditioned by probability, opportunism and relativity, *believing* warranted *being*. "Making believe," by constructing the contingent verisimilitudes that supported communal action, was the sole purpose of public speech. Sophistic confidence bound together and energized all who sought the reins of power. It supplanted superstition, tradition and the advantages of birth as the primary determinant of personal fulfillment and self-realization. It recast the relationship between individual being and social character. A person was no longer simply the member of a family or a tribe. He was a citizen of the city and, as such, paradoxically became both a political concretion and a philosophical abstraction. The sophistic epistemology sought to link the concrete and the abstract through written laws, civic charters and political constitutions. Through what political thinkers of the 18th century would call the "social compact," the sophists supplied the necessary intellectual framework to harness and channel the animal emotions of human beings in competitive proximity. They supported, that is, the notion of progressive civilization. Sophistic rhetoric

grew out of the need to commune with fellow citizens, to provide a basis for agreement and action that would lead to the
fulfillment of the common good.

Such was the charter of the *polis*. It may have risen out of the
need for defense or protection, but it reached its greatest potential as an instrument for the cultivation of the human spirit. In
such a view of life in community, persuasion assumes a validity
external to the acts of suasive speech or argumentative logic.
The sophist stood in front of his audience and addressed them
directly, eye to eye. His success or failure was measured by his
ability to fulfill the expectations he raised as a thinker as well as
a speaker. His primary goal was to translate ideas into actions.

Now, however, individual success is largely measured by
wealth and material plenty. More often than not it is attained
despite the intrusion of politics into our private affairs. Indeed,
we abhor politics and politicians. Public life has been at once
abandoned and professionalized. Our own sophistication has
trained us to beware of the man or woman who seeks fulfillment outside his or her own self. Our politicians are seen for
what they are, cold and calculating, self-consumed, egotistical,
at times histrionic, always opportunistic, rarely candid, never
trustworthy. Aristotle's transformation of politics and rhetoric
into arts of possibility and probability finds no home in the
world of action. They are relegated to the academic realm.
Plato's ideal state can be found in the utopian visions that arise
from time to time as a proposed solution to our earthly cares.
Platonisms enliven opposites and, in keeping with the paradoxical nature of the times, they can support the fundamentalist
reactions to modern culture as well as the technological dreams
of futurists and other professional visionaries.

By revolutionizing the way we communicate with each other,
television has transformed politics and altered the role each of
us plays in it. Where the Greek was an active participant in
political affairs, a citizen whose power existed in proportion to
his ability to speak before his fellows, we are passive consumers
of political images. Politics is now a spectator sport periodically
more important than football or baseball. We even describe it as
a contest, pay close attention to its advances and reversals,

divide ourselves into different teams, simplify its subtleties through polls and projections, decry its abuses, bankroll its processes, vivify its personalities, ignore its substance, avoid its institutions and, with increasing frequency, abstain from its elections. Politicians are celebrities valued for their pleasing personalities rather than their penetrating minds, admirable characters, spontaneous intelligence or unique vision. They court constituencies through prepackaged appeals. The electorate is an amorphous herd to be subdivided and addressed on the basis of demographic differences rather than democratic similarities.

Debate is now conducted by means of images rather than by the opposed verbal arguments that articulate coherent trains of thought. These images are targeted at specific emotions held by particular segments of the polity. They are intended to arouse, exaggerate and reinforce feelings and fears that can be made to serve as the basis for judgment and action. The images of modern politics are reality itself, devoid of any context except that which they themselves provide. They exist for a passing moment, framed against the luminescent backdrop of an ever-changing, stage-managed political drama scripted for the cold eye of the television camera.

The ancient sophist thought he was liberating the mind to compete amid the cacophony of democracy. He stood before the mob and by speaking eloquently and perhaps with passion transformed it into an instrument of change. He used his person, his being, his body and his voice to construct a temporary reality based on his confidence in his power to move others to act. The modern sophist despises free thought. He rarely appears in person, preferring to work instead behind the scenes, as advisor or instructor to the candidate. In the ancient world, technique and intention united in the person of the sophist. The public persona of the modern politician more often than not merely represents rather than embodies the thoughts it puts into language. The modern sophist is usually a communication specialist who seeks control. He also knows, as one presidential media adviser has put it, that "visuals" outlast the spoken word. A picture is worth thousands of votes. Rhetoric has become an art of visual appeal whose logic is based not on the induction or deduction of finely wrought arguments but, rather, on the seduction of carefully selected images. Aristotle's art has been reduced to the trivialities he found in ancient sophistry. It still appeals exclusively to the emotions, but it spurns even language as the mode of communication. Appearance is reality.

The use of imagery is not haphazard. It flows from an ongoing process of sampling and analyzing public opinion through a variety of techniques, most notably polling and the use of focus groups. Both have evolved into a quasi-science that analyzes responses to certain key messages and constructs appeals guaranteed to have the desired effect. It is a commonplace of our time that politics is packaged and marketed like every other commodity in a consumer society. What is not so clearly understood is that these techniques reverse the traditional rhetorical concept of public persuasion which assumed that an audience needs to be unified and led from known, commonly accepted truths to less known, less accepted opinions. Leaders now follow the crowd, arriving at key points in its confused march to common opinion in order to appear to have gotten there first. Politicians seek to capitalize on those moments when events, images and the prejudices of the audience can be brought into alignment in order to convey a pre-tested, appropriately packaged message. To be foreknowing is to be forearmed.

Polls, focus groups and other public opinion research—ostensibly "objective" methods for determining public opinion—are the basis for deciding "factness" in a world where factuality itself is continually called into question. Great pains are taken to craft this research, to factor out the inessentials and to focus on the nuances of belief and prejudice that the candidate can act upon. The focus group, where a dozen or so participants are gathered to talk about selected topics or techniques, is less a conversation where opinions emerge than a choosing between several alternatives. It is a favorite device nowadays because, at one level, it projects the aura of give-and-take. The focus group pretends to be the purest of dialectics. In actuality, it is not a dialogue at all, where views are modified, accepted or rejected. Rather, it is a directed, cushioned discussion. Participants report that they are often hurried to conclusions or fed statements—

interpretations and paraphrases really—of their own opinions and then asked to verify or reject the characterization.

This relentless seeking of opinion and shaping of bias has transformed politics. Socrates and Protagoras explored each other's ideas by direct contact, argumentative assertion, dialectical analysis, sophistic refutation and logical reconstruction. They engaged in a free-flowing discussion of alternatives. Demosthenes and Aeschines confronted each other in person before a relatively stable group of auditors who could be swayed first one way then another by the stream of argument. Socrates, Protagoras, Demosthenes and Aeschines would find cold comfort in the modern techniques of sophisticated political analysis.

Ours is a politics by remote control. The sophists of our age are rarely those who stand before the crowd. There is no modern equivalent to Demosthenes, the inspired and inspiring orator who can whip an audience to action through sheer force of personality and the appeal of a single voice. We would call that demagoguery. Indeed, it is doubtful whether he could survive a medium that values everywhere the cool, dispassionate and self-assured image. Reality is not enough anymore. Political news is boring, or so it is said, and must be enlivened. Conflict, corruption and scandal, preferably involving large sums of money and women of innocent but enticing beauty, are more popular than contemplating the future of the republic. Ours is an age of great simplification that values the appearance of better living through imagistic manipulation.

For all the Machiavellian intricacy that sophisticated politics entails, the public self projected by a political leader must not be complicated. Indeed, as Ronald Reagan proved, it is more effective if it is not. Yet success in politics is not without its paradoxes. The political verisimilitude obscures and even obliterates the character of the politician. The paradox of Ronald Reagan is that while he believed in and practiced that things are only as they seem to be, he left behind a nation wondering if something else was going on. He was a born-again conservative who admired Franklin Roosevelt. He campaigned against big government and governed in a manner that doubled our public indebtedness on its behalf. He spoke militantly against our major adversary and ended up admiring its leader. He spoke often and piously of religious values but rarely practiced any faith. In a word, he was the supreme expression of sophistication, a contradictory man who projected a pleasing, reassuring image that gave the rest of us permission to preach one thing and practice another. Image is real in sophistic culture. Selfhood is not. *Where's the Rest of Me?* is not only an ironically apt title for Ronald Reagan's first autobiography, published in 1965. It also stands as the paradoxical epigram for the political self.

Ronald Reagan's great talent, to appear in command even when things are spinning out of control, is every politicians great challenge. *Appearing* carries the same weight as *being*. That is why the modern presidency depends as much for its success on "media advisors," "spin doctors" and "handlers" as it does on the character of the person who happens to be president. Words, arguments and images are the symbolic manifestation of an arbitrarily determined reality. Sophisticated culture is self-inventing.

For that reason, the extensive commentary by media news personalities about the lack of substance in our politicians is at best ironic. Not only are the commentators themselves but flickering, incorporeal images to most of us. Those images are only made real by the context of controversy they perpetuate, the peculiar hunger of television for pictures rather than words. The image is substance, a principle well known to the telecommunications industry that drives our politics. The ghosts of television news are always playing on the duality of rhetorical self-consciousness. They have no choice. The medium of their communication relentlessly shows only the surface of the world, the mere appearances. The disembodied voice-over often tells us that reality lurks somewhere beneath or behind or beyond the images we see. Television may mirror the national self in all its complexity. But it also creates the myriad impressions and perceptions and points of view that, in their totality, constitute the American ethos.

Our attention constantly shifts to matters of seemingly greater concern, which we always examine in the isolation of the pervasive present. But they demand to be seen in the context of our sophistication and the effects it has on our ability to conceive and express them. For the ancient distinction between speaker, speech and subject matter has collapsed. The new instruments of mass communication blur the line between the image, the message and the messenger. Like the captive souls in Plato's cave we are never certain of the reality of the shadows that parade before us on the wall.

Because they are central to our daily understanding of ourselves and of others, the new instruments of communication determine the quality of life in its broadest sense. Television, satellites and computers simultaneously embody and propagate sophistic concepts about image and reality throughout the world. Sophistication is a global phenomenon rooted in two unique aspects of American culture, technological innovation and consumer economics. Electronic instruments of mass communication are inventions of our time, but sophistic culture has always been popular and pervasive. America has become the "school of the world," a phrase first used to describe the Athens of Pericles. It is also the world's marketplace and armory. American concepts and techniques of suasive communication are picked up, adapted and transformed by other societies organized around different concepts of community, commonwealth and citizenship. As Athens was shaped by the reflection of its own sophistication back on itself, so too modern America is constantly reacquiring in changed form and function her previously exported rhetorical techniques of management, politics and technical innovation. They flow across our borders, back and forth, in an endless evolutionary stream of ideas and practices. Politics and rhetoric have emerged triumphant in the latter half of the 20th century, borne on the physics of the electron. National boundaries are thin defenses against the penetrating power of electronic mass communication. The Berlin Wall was finally destroyed not by the picks and hammers of an irate people but by the relentless penetration of microwaves bearing glad tidings from the West.

The sophistication of international politics and its accompanying paradoxes are clearly seen in the phenomenon of Mikhail Gorbachev, whose so-called public relations successes cannot be explained adequately without reference to the techniques of persuasion practiced by American marketers and politicians. Soviet foreign policy, once dogmatic and predictable, now evolves around detailed assessments of world opinion and the calculation of immediate domestic political effects versus long term strategic goals. It is communicated in language, images and forms familiar and acceptable to Western audiences. Indeed, it is broadcast over the heads of a Soviet citizenry more concerned with bread and work than with world peace. Above all, Soviet foreign policy heeds an important principle of sophistication. Energetic self-assertion by photogenic and appealing personalities powerfully affects the attitudes and opinions of the sophisticated Western mind. Well-groomed English-speaking Kremlin representatives have replaced the gray-suited, somber, unflinching Soviet diplomats of a decade ago. The substitution signals a dawning awareness of the fact that the pleasing personality is central to the successful execution of modern video politics.

The public perception of all kinds of organizations, nations and institutions as well as corporations and local political communities, is drawn from the perceived qualities of their leaders. Once a culture becomes sophisticated, traditional instruments of suasion and control no longer pertain to the changed circumstances. Troops can be sent in and repressive measures reinstituted, but the exercise of the old ways of power eventually lead to the downfall of the oppressor. Modern political sophistication pivots on the personality of leaders and the opinions of an engaged population. Populism becomes the key to power, and it must always be demonstrated in at least a seemingly, if not actual, democratic manner. Pericles, after all, exercised one man rule in the guise of popular politics.

The pursuit of politics involves the constant redefinition and reorganization of "community" in its most esoteric sense. At one level, it is a theoretical pursuit, the realm of thinkers who seek to improve on the models of actuality by projecting causes and effects into an uncertain future. Not surprisingly, the modern proponents of Plato's *Politeia* are the science fiction writers and film-makers who seek analogies to the present in fantastic communities of the distant past or future. Their worlds tend to exemplify pragmatic thinking gone wrong. Genetic experimentation, unbridled exploitation of distant planets, the subjugation of different species or the corruption of political power on a galactic scale, all express deep seated utopian anxieties about the implications of political realities on Earth in the here and now. At another level, the reorganization of community—the search after the principle of social order—is embodied in the practical sciences of politics and rhetoric as they are taught in the schools. The modern proponents of Aristotle's *Politics* are the professors of -ologies and -isms. They come in many guises, as economist, sociologist, or political scientist. They differ according to how they look at the world and what they see, but they are united by a shared confidence in the power of the logic of differentiation and classification to reveal the motive causes of human events. Their systems and sciences and programs of study reflect an anxiety with the unpredictable nature of politics, of the uncertainties of human nature itself.

But the theoretical and the practical are joined in the practice of politics itself, not just as the on-going reorganization of community or the search for the principle of social order, but in the formation of individual being and its expression in social character. Every sentient being is a politician so mixed of the ancient traditions and tendencies that we hardly know ourselves, much less others. Each of us is Platonist in our promises, Aristotelian in our programs and Demosthenean in our performances. It is our culture that makes us so. For the difference between the three ancient positions of Plato, Aristotle and Demosthenes is left unresolved in our time. We do not see them as contradictions or as alternatives. For us, they merely represent the continuum of reality that exists for the mind seeking itself. In our sophisticated age, the discord between thought, expression and action is taken as a sign of the richness of life, of the fullness of human potentiality. We move easily between the promise and the practice of politics, cynical about both but trusting ultimately in our own ability to discern the operational truth among all the fictions and fallacies. The contingent verisimilitude is the highest order of reality in the sophisticated age. And politics is the highest form of verisimilitude. It is the realm of life where "seeming to be" reaches the fullest expression in its public manifestation. The power of sophisticated politics resides in the power of the individual mind to fashion for itself, and for others, a basis for judgment and action. Politics consists not only of ignoring the facts but of inventing them as well.

The Power of Sophisticated Politics

CHAPTER FOUR

Learning to Act:
The Paradox of
Sophisticated Education

*Any education given by a group tends to socialize its
members, but the quality and value of the socialization
depends upon the habits and aims of the group.*
—John Dewey

THE INTERPLAY BETWEEN individual being and social character not only determines history and enlivens politics, it
also energizes the various programs of study that constitute education. Indeed, the invention of the past and the search
for community in an ever-changing present create special circumstances for the formation and transmission of knowledge.
Education attempts to harness the past and the present to produce a communal future that is expressed at any given moment
in the habits, actions, attitudes and aspirations of each individual citizen.

The fundamental questions about the origins and content of
knowledge—What do we know? How do we know that we
know? How do we tell (or demonstrate or portray or communicate) what we know?—serve as the commonplaces for markedly
different educational programs, each of which purports to deliver
the individual into some state of improved being or greater
awareness or increased ability. And despite the apparent novelty

of contemporary innovations in our schools, we borrow terms, concepts, methods, and arts from the Greeks and Romans to fashion a system of democratic education that underwrites the essential values of sophistic culture. Moreover, although the central epistemological questions of contemporary education can be stated briefly, they have persistently puzzled philosophers of every kind from Plato to the present.

In part, the three epistemological questions are historical. They attempt to locate the foundations of knowledge within a flow of human invention that can be traced from some arbitrarily determined past to the always-tentative, pervasive present. Our search for knowledge invariably involves an interpretive dialogue between a self-consciously inquiring mind and the artifacts left behind by the thinking beings who have come before us. Although that dialogue may at times appear quaint and self-concerned, like the talk of a shy antiquarian at a university cocktail party, it is necessarily connected to the pragmatic circumstances of living fully in the present.

Then again, the ancient questions about the origins and transmission of knowledge are also political, in the wider sense of the word. The epistemological quest forces each mind into an argumentative interaction with the manifold constituents of the surrounding social environment—other people, ideas, and expressions of reality. Because our times are characterized both by rapid change and by an abundance of disciplines that claim to reveal the underlying truths of commonplace life, the social environment is fragmented, diffuse and incoherent. Democratic society lacks a natural authoritative center. It derives its cultural meaning, its social sense, from the sensibilities of competing, often conflicting and sometimes cooperating individual minds. Our search for knowledge involves a conscious, continuous reordering of the data of everyday experience by means of argument, assertion, declaration, and debate as well as through the agency of casual conversation. The assertive dialogue of the self-conscious mind appears slick and opportunistic, like the rehearsed speech of the politician running for office. Yet along with our reflection on things past, our self-conscious claims about reality are absolutely essential to life in the present tense.

History and politics—the invented past and the ever-inventive present—serve to locate one's unique self within the context of many other selves. Neither the historical nor the political sensibility, however, constitutes self-realization in its entirety. Coming to terms with one's self also entails coming to terms with the fragmented circumstances, the disparate communities and the invented histories of our culture. Self-knowledge requires the structured environment of education. Even then, what is revealed to the educated mind represents only a partial view of things.

Education serves many purposes. It links history and politics, as subject matters as well as social forces. It transmits knowledge and values from one generation to another. It establishes the parameters of social organization and determines the limits of individual behavior within them. And it legitimizes thought and expression. Education cultivates an appreciation of the mind's many products, whether they be material, intellectual, organizational, commercial, technological, or moral. It encourages the exploration of ideas and abstractions as if they possessed real meaning for the world of concrete action. Education is the mortar that binds together history, politics, ethics and aesthetics as the primary constituents of culture.

Our views about education and the controversies that surround them are rooted, like so much else in modern culture, in the ancient past. We are self-conscious heirs to ideas, concepts, methods, systems and strategies of learning that can be traced to Plato, Aristotle and the sophists, who together set the terms for the discussion of the central role played by knowledge and learning in communal life. They each sought to place the consciousness of history, power, creativity, virtue and beauty within some scheme that could be passed from one mind to another with unobstructed clarity. Purposeful and direct, education makes possible the persistence through time of eternal ideas and links one generation with another though centuries may intervene between the two. Human understanding thus assumes both an individual and a social nature, for it can only exist as the product of the reflexive relationship between language and reality. That relationship, in turn, was conceived by the ancients around differing concepts of rhetoric.

In Periclean Athens, first the sophists and then their rivals attempted to reorder culture by reforming the education of the young. Gorgias, Protagoras and Hippias gained popularity because they offered courses of study that seemed to suit the practical needs of life in an emerging, argumentative democracy. They emphasized the social nature of the human being and developed curricula that promised to transform any person into an effective public performer. Rhetoric became the sole focus of their curriculum although its methods and functions were transmuted into other subject matters to serve a variety of ends.

Plato and Aristotle proposed ornate epistemological constructions to redress the perceived deficiencies of an exclusively rhetorical sophistic education. Plato struck at the moral relativity of rhetoric and its characteristic emphasis on affectation, pretense and guile. He rejected rhetoric as nothing more than specious reasoning and mere flattery. His student Aristotle, however, sought the grounds of knowledge that could produce sciences and arts to rival the truncated rhetoric of the sophists. He reformed the rhetorical impulse of the sophists and gave it a system, a goal and perhaps most important, a psychology. The terms sophist and sophistry carry pejorative meanings today because Plato and Aristotle both had a stake in distinguishing their own intellectual enterprises from those of the sophists. Both attacked sophistry by reference to rhetoric and dialectic, although they differed as to the nature and use of these arts. In turn, those differences animated fundamentally unique streams of thought that can be only grossly distinguished as "Platonist" or "Aristotelian." These flow into our own age in many guises as distinct philosophic impulses, discrete systems of thought and diverse methods of analysis and judgment. They also come down to us as solutions to the paradoxes of sophistic education.

Plato's critique of sophists and sophistry was initiated in defense of Socrates, who was put to death by his fellow Athenians for being a sophist in deed if not in name. The confusion was understandable given the peculiar role Socrates chose to play as the self-appointed curmudgeon of Athens. He was the first Western mind to focus speculative thought on the attainment of the virtuous life in community. He inquired after the nature of good and evil, right and wrong, truth and falsity, appearance and reality, by means of dialectic. In the hands of Socrates, dialectic was a method of investigation that posed conflicting assertions about the nature of something and attempted to resolve the contradiction by definition, classification and deductive reasoning. Socrates was accused of sophistry because dialectic resembled sophistic disputation and often led to the same results, the devastation of an opponent's position through the inversion of the original terms of his argument. Socrates was expert at turning matters on their head, showing in the process that things are rarely as they seem to be.

The Platonic dialogues featuring Socrates at once portray and embody the rightful use of dialectical method. Founded on the give and take of argument and the inclination of every human being toward self-discovery, dialectical inquiry leads its participants to glimpse the supreme grounding for virtuous action. In Plato's hands, dialectical reasoning became more than a method of debate, and it even exceeded its broader charge to inquire after the nature of things. It served as a way of *perceiving* the world of human beings and their behavior. Dialectic is an animated and active art, directed always at the souls of those who engage it.

For Plato, dialectic overwhelms the mere tinkering of the sophists, who played at dialectical debate but actually used many of the baser techniques of rhetorical persuasion to gain advantage in the law courts and the public assemblies. The better speaker, rather than the better reasoner, often won in these arenas. The sophists promised to transform the common man into an uncommon leader of public opinion. According to Plato, however, they practiced a sham art. Sophists dealt not with fundamental realities but with fictive illusions created by the skillful manipulation of language and emotions. Only dialectical inquiry penetrates the veil of emotive language to reveal, if only briefly, the substantial unchanging truth that is merely projected by objects in the material world. In short, Plato developed Socratic self-doubt into a manifold and intricate scheme for the investigation of all sorts of questions about the right-minded behavior of individual beings and the proper development of social character.

Aristotle accepted the need to provide an explicable framework for humane knowledge. As the founder of a school that differed with Plato on fundamental questions about reality, he spent his life working out the intricate connections within and among clearly defined disciplines of inquiry, theory and practice. Aristotle's reaction to the sophists is characteristically different from Plato's. He recognized that properly conceived and directed, the dialectical and rhetorical elements of sophistic thought have a place in the construction of all systematic science and art. His innovation was to work these impulses into a formal epistemology, where they both enliven and focus the distinction between the true and false premises of organized, scientific knowledge. Rhetoric and dialectic operate at the level of personal belief in Aristotle's scheme of things. They represent the first of several stages for evaluating common opinions about any matter. Dialectic and rhetoric are *architectonic* arts that structure the inquiry into the premises of every field of knowledge. Ultimately, in the progress of science, they are surpassed by the certainties of analytic research and discourse and the formal categories of logic. They fit into a continuum of arts and sciences that are to be distinguished in the first instance by the fealty of thought to expression, of causes to effects.

According to Aristotle, the sophists knew only a part of rhetoric, the power of emotional appeals. They were ignorant of its capacity to invent and order coherent lines of argument. And they had no notion of its relationship to the subject matters of other disciplines. Sophistic is a general technique, where argumentation depends on the manipulation of words and the accidents of association. It is unrestrained by the need to reproduce the opinions of men or to reflect the nature of things. Aristotle's rhetoric, however, along with its sister art dialectic, "base their arguments on the opinions of men," which are, in turn, the basis of an intricate, artful process of sophistication that leads paradoxically from uncertainty to certainty, from things alleged to things proved. Moreover, "the nature of things" encompasses the basis of reality itself. The sophist invents *ex nihilo*, out of nothing, and deals in airy abstractions. Aristotle's rhetorician, however, treats the very essences of life.

Dialectic and rhetoric deal with a peculiar class of logical constructions, the enthymeme and the example, which can be analyzed solely as instruments of probability. Dialectic covers the topical structures of argument while rhetoric encompasses the circumstances determining topical analysis and argumentation. Once rhetoric moves into the social or political realm, however, an ethical test can be made concerning the consequences of action. The rhetorician ponders not only the tactics of moving people to act but also the *rightness* of exercising his power to move them in the first place. He considers the consequences of his actions by reference to ethics, a subject of inquiry with its own special class of problems and methods. Aristotle's rhetorician reflects on human behavior in terms of self-confidence and self-doubt.

Both the Platonic and the Aristotelian views of rhetoric and dialectic support complex, crucially different, educational systems. In Plato, dialectic is at once the best method of inquiry, the highest kind of knowledge and the most beautiful form of expression. It subsumes all other arts into its threefold magnificence. In Aristotle, rhetoric and dialectic are *universal* arts differing in both form and content from Plato's abstract universality. Although they lack specific content as arts, they are applicable to the subject matter of any other art. They are neither "higher" nor "lower" than the other arts and sciences. They are merely distinguished by their means, manner and ends. They are part, that is, of an integrated hierarchical epistemology that moves from sense to science, from common opinion to demonstrated fact.

Plato's *Politeia* proposes an educational system for the perfect state that reflects the social and intellectual distinctions of its citizens. The *polis* is divided into three classes. Foremost are the rulers, who are responsible for both the theory and practice of government. Next are the guardians whose duty it is to protect the community and to maintain public order. Finally, there are the common people—herders, craftsmen, traders, laborers—

who furnish the material necessities of life for all the citizens. Although Plato spends little time describing the lowest class he does not exclude them from elementary education; their work is necessary to the community. Plato's *Politeia* is at heart a communist society. It operates by the radically egalitarian dictum that has inspired similar utopian arrangements in our own time: from each according to his ability, to each according to his need. It is in this context that Plato distinguishes three stages of education. The first, open to all citizens, reflects the conventional education of Plato's Athens. It consists of "music for the mind and gymnastic for the body." *Music*, to be studied between the ages ten to seventeen, includes literature and what we call the "liberal arts." It precedes the study of *gymnastic*, or systematic physical training, which occupies the years between seventeen and twenty. In Plato's *Politeia*, as opposed to the actual practice in Athens, careful attention is paid to the environment as well as to the subject of study. Beauty is to dominate everywhere, nothing mean or ugly must meet the eye or ear of the student. The Platonic system is at heart one of immersion and osmosis. The fairy tales of childhood, along with the other fantastic products of the poets, are under strict censorship. Only that which represents good deeds, honest men and the truth in general can be taught. The music must be martial, the art and literature representative, the physical activity pragmatic, the ideology communal. Plato's first stage of education links morality and aesthetics, the virtuous with the beautiful.

At the age of twenty, the most promising students are chosen to spend the next ten years studying the sciences, which Plato understood to include arithmetic, geometry, astronomy and harmony. All these serve to develop and hone the intellect by forcing the mind to work rigorously within the strictures of well-founded principles and theorems. The major benefit of science in Plato's *Politeia* is that it contributes to the disciplining of the mind.

Only after the student has progressed through this level can he (or she, since Plato's *Politeia* is unique among ancient treatises for its emphasis on the equality of the sexes) qualify for the five-year study of dialectic, the highest form of knowledge in

Plato's educational system. It is at this point that the student is permitted to engage in philosophic speculation. Plato felt that early exposure to the less precise disciplines of philosophy and politics would damage the student's ability to think clearly, since these areas of thought lead away from precision and into the murkiness of worldly confusions. Dialectical training requires maturity and a healthy sense of irony. At thirty-five, the person who has passed through training in dialectic is fit for the highest position in public life. At fifty, he may retire to devote himself to further study of philosophy.

The first stage of Plato's system is open to nearly all citizens. The second stage is open only to members of the guardians and the rulers. The third stage of education, however, is intended for a small group out of which emerges the *philosopher-king*. In its progression from the many to the few to the One, the stages of education in Plato's ideal state reflect the increasing centrality of dialectic to the educational purpose. It is a winnowing and honing process intended to render the uniquely singular mind of the philosopher king fit enough to lead the rest of the community. It is thus a rational system in the most elementary sense of the term; it seeks to eliminate accidents and errors from the educational regimen. We have difficulty understanding why Plato banishes poets and fabulists from his *Politeia*, but in his terms the banishment of all those who deal in fictions, lies and misrepresentations makes sense. After all, dialectic aims to uncover the substantial nature of things. It treats language as a veil to be pierced, not as a mask to be used for entertainment or suasion or even education. The aesthetic and the moral converge. It is the business of the state to invent for educational purposes specifically moral myths and tales, and to substitute them for the fabulous stories it has rejected. Imitation is an important and undeniable aspect of human nature, Plato would admit, in seeming agreement with the sophists. But it lacks a sufficient supply of ideal characterizations in art. If imitation is to be harnessed, then the wise leaders of the state must become the sources for thoughts and actions to be imitated. They, rather than the gods and men of the *Iliad*, for example, must serve as fit material for study and copying. Imitated *and* imitating, the philosopher-king exercises strict control over the imitative arts. Plato's educational system serves a truly moral purpose. It aims ultimately at unity of appearance and reality, thought and expression, mind and matter, and of the true, the good and the beautiful.

Like Plato, Aristotle takes language seriously. He understands it to be a natural phenomenon and at times seems to suggest that it is even a material event. Language not only expresses what we know. It embodies knowledge itself. It is a cause of effects. And it brings into being what would never exist without it. Where Plato is suspicious of the power of language to ordain and order reality, Aristotle accepts its potency as a fact of life. Like the sophists, he finds in the human ability to create and use language that special characteristic which distinguishes us from the other animals and gives us dominion over them.

Aristotle's educational theories are formulated in several places, but they all emanate from the simple principle which opens his *Metaphysics*. "All men by nature desire to know," he writes, and language is both the instrument and product of knowing. This desire to know goes well beyond simple curiosity. It eventually encompasses three realms of science—theoretical, practical and poetic (or productive)—that are distinguishable by their aims and by their certainty. Theoretical science aims to reveal knowledge itself. It entails the accumulation and understanding of first principles that pass for "knowing" in its purest, simplest form. Practical science aims to produce appropriate behavior. It entails knowledge that leads to "doing" or "acting." And the poetic science aims at composition or construction or production, at knowledge that results in "making." Since theoretical science deals with what usually or always happens, it claims the highest degree of certainty. The practical and poetic sciences, on the other hand, are focused on action or production, on "doing" something. Consequently, they cannot be judged by the strict criteria of truth or certainty. Instead, they are measured by their effectiveness in disclosing the best means for bringing about what is to be done or made or performed. The practical and the poetic sciences thus provide rules of conduct and rules of art that guide our effective actions. They are not expositions of the *truth* however conceived.

The distinction between the three kinds of knowledge is critical to Aristotle's conception of education as an activity of socialization conducted within the intellectual, social, moral and, most important, political milieu of the state. Like Plato, Aristotle accepts the *polis* as the best unit of government. Also like Plato, he speculates on the role of education in producing a citizenry supportive of the ideal state. Education should be systematic and regulated. It is too important to be left to individual caprice. Education is the only method for instilling virtue as a Greek would conceive of it, as *arete* or excellence in form, purpose and action. Although an individual may benefit from private education, owing to the greater contact between teacher and student, it is nevertheless important for the state to control the curriculum of the schools. After all, it is through education that the state ultimately attains its ends, to preserve and promote the commonwealth. For this reason, education ought to be both uniform and general since the state may need to call upon every citizen to take a share of the responsibility for government. Aristotle also agrees with Plato on the division of education into two periods, separated by an interval devoted to physical training.

There, however, the similarities end. Plato's theory of education is based on the assumption that all learning is a process of reminiscence, the recovery of innate ideas (present at birth) by means of dialectical inquiry. Aristotle, however, grounds knowledge in the senses, with the mind progressing from sensation through memory and experience to knowledge. Consequently, Aristotle's ideal state is less regimented than Plato's. It recognizes that the *polis* is a dynamic, organic invention of human genius, not the static expression of an ideal form. The end of education is for each man to learn to employ leisure in the best possible way. Contemplation, the exercise of the highest functions of the intellect, offers the best opportunity to attain the most excellent form of life possible. From the exercise of intellectual power, man derives happiness. It is this goal, and not the social efficiency of Plato's *Politeia*, that animates the educational efforts of both the individual being and the well-ordered state.

Plato and Aristotle have left us detailed descriptions of

education in the ideal state. They have also left a body of literature that, directly and indirectly, discusses issues pertaining to
educational theory. The sophists, however, have left us nothing
in the way of formal treatises. In fact, we know of their essential
positions only from the works Plato, Aristotle and other writers
have composed in reaction to them. We also possess the writings of contemporaries such as Isocrates, who focused closely
on teaching rhetoric and oratory and yet is to be distinguished
from the other prominent sophists of the day as well as from
Plato and Aristotle. From Isocrates it is possible to deduce the
broad outline of sophistic education.

The Greek sophist professed a pragmatic art and sophistic
pedagogy took up where formal education left off. It was peculiarly responsive to the social environment which conditions
education in any culture. Perhaps the single most significant
cause of the sophistication of Greek culture was the constitu-
tional reform of the Athenian leader Solon who, in the sixth
century B.C., mandated that all citizens be schooled in reading
and writing, essential skills of a democracy increasingly reliant
on written laws. Solon's reforms created not only codified law,
but also the necessity to argue persuasively about the origin and
meaning of legal texts and the means by which every Athenian
could acquire legal expertise. Since formal education, however,
fell short of teaching how to use these skills to personal advantage in the realms of public life, the sophists stepped in to fill the
need. They understood both the innate human desire to improve one's lot and the opportunities democratic government
offered for the promotion of one's self. In a political environment where words and images carry the most weight, success
went to those who could move others to act. Consequently,
according to both the sophists and their detractors, the ancient
courses in disputation, argumentation and dialectic aimed to
make the weaker argument the stronger, the lesser need the
greater, and the unfamiliar opinion the more common, all with
the end in mind of causing things to happen according to the
dramatized intentions of the speaker. If man is the measure of
all things, as Protagoras averred, then it is man the *actor* who sets
the standard for other human beings.

Isocrates gives the best description of the sophistic pedagogy, albeit from a critical position. He was born in 436 B.C. and
lived to see the independent Greek *polis* absorbed into the larger
political organization of Philip of Macedon (Alexander the
Great's father) after his victory at Chaeronea, in 338 B.C. Unlike
the proselytizing sophists, Isocrates never lectured to large audiences, preferring instead to instruct no more than two students
at a time. His course of study was based on a broad conception
of rhetorical composition that reflected a philosophic outlook
though he himself was no philosopher. What he calls "philosophy" is a theory of culture. It reflects the Athens of his day, a
tumultuous, talkative, turbulent place where the articulate ruled,
the eloquent commanded, and silence was construed as consent. The philosophy of Isocrates, like that of the sophists, was
reached through a discipline of public discourse that bears on
the practical life. He opened a school of rhetoric in Athens in 392
B.C. and is generally reckoned as one of the great Athenian
rhetoricians, though he seldom spoke in public. He was not so
much an orator as a teacher and writer of orations for delivery
by others. His life spans the rise and collapse of the Golden Age,
and so encompasses Plato's lifetime and a good part of Aristotle's
as well.

Unlike Plato and Aristotle, Isocrates indicts the professional
educators of Athens as a colleague, according to distinctions in
subject matter and end. His criticism appears in two speeches
separated by 35 years. The first, *Against the Sophists*, survives only
in fragments, and is intended to prepare the way for a statement
of his own theory. That earlier statement is missing, but the
second speech, *On the Antidosis*, a defense of his life and profession, contains a well-developed educational theory. Although
Isocrates criticizes the narrow practice of most sophists, he pro-
pounds a vision of education that is neither Platonist nor Aristotelian. Rather, it is "sophistic" in its highest form. His treatise,
then, is in some measure an antidote to the criticisms of both
Plato and Aristotle as well as to the excesses of his fellow
professional educators.

Isocrates' complaint against the sophists is simple: they
promise more than they can deliver. He discerns three classes of

sophistic teachers, each of which is marked by its own excesses and deficiencies. First, there are the professors of disputation, or "eristic," who promise to impart to their pupils a knowledge of right conduct which can lead to perfect happiness. They sell this gift for what Isocrates considers a ridiculously small fee (he believed in charging market rates, and more). This attack is not aimed at the class of sophists Plato denounces but, rather, at the followers of Socrates known as the Megarians, itinerants who applied the dialectic for worldly gain under the pretense of seeking the eternal truths.

The next class of sophists with whom Isocrates finds fault are the teachers of political discourse, the professors of practical rhetoric. These care nothing for the truth, Isocrates charges, which at least the eristics professed to pursue. The chief aim of the teachers of political discourse, however, is to attract students by specious promises. They claim to be able to teach oratory as easily as the alphabet to anyone who can pay the fee. This runs contrary to Isocrates' own views that natural ability, theoretical training and experience are the primary constituents of successful oratory. And of these, the first is by far the most important. Nothing a sophist teaches, no matter the fee he charges, can supply to the student what nature leaves out.

Finally, there are the compilers of technical handbooks. These writers conceive of rhetoric as a technical art, thereby missing what for Isocrates is its underlying power and psychology. Worse still, they invariably instruct in litigation, a thing Isocrates finds offensive in itself. As a class of sophists, the handbook writers are lower than the eristics, who at least pretend to be concerned with virtue and moderation. The only motive of the technical rhetoricians, though, is greed and covetousness. Their work is one important cause, according to Isocrates, for the decline in the quality of public discourse.

From his criticisms, it is possible to see how Isocrates differs from Plato and Aristotle. Plato's critique is levelled against sophists in general and, as we have seen, takes particular issue with their underlying epistemology. Aristotle's critique is closer to Isocrates' in that he also takes issue with the manner and end of the art of rhetoric they propound. However, Aristotle wants to move rhetoric into the spectrum of all arts and science and, along with dialectic, to give it a circumscribed role in the foundation of knowledge, the examination of opinions and the articulation of principles. Isocrates' motives are more modest than those of either Plato or Aristotle and at the same time more ambitious than those of the lesser sophists. For him, life is lived on the ground. Philosophy does for the soul what gymnastics does for the body; it is a propaedeutic exercise that strengthens the intellect for the tasks at hand. Natural ability may be the most important element of success, but instruction and practice are indispensable. Perseverance is the highest virtue, since the regimen of proper sophistic training can extend over many years and involves great dedication and difficult labor. Absolute knowledge—either as a principle of virtuous behavior or of true enlightenment—is unattainable. Instead, the wise man can make a satisfactory guess about what needs to be done and can understand the consequences of action.

Like many of the great sophists Isocrates was a pan-Hellenist. Unlike Plato or Aristotle, his world was not defined by the *polis* alone. His concern for education as a social phenomenon did not seek to reinforce citizen loyalties or a sense of duty. It was pragmatic and hard-boiled. It is no accident that Isocrates regarded the rise of a strong Macedonia as the essential element for the unification of all Greece. In his view, this pan-Hellenic union greatly increased the need for a population schooled in civic discourse. Rhetoric was the only art that promised to speak across the traditional barriers between city-states, to unite the Greeks as a people in language as well as in fact.

As a preparation for his own courses in rhetoric, he insisted that his pupils learn grammar and poetry, which was the custom of the time. Later, mathematics and even eristics would be studied because they provided good mental training and produced supple, facile intellects. His own method was to instruct his pupils in all styles of prose composition, just as the gymnastic master starts with the basic moves of his craft before proceeding to the most difficult. After suitable practice and proven proficiency with the known forms of expression, the student composed his own exercises on topics carefully chosen to cover a wide range of subjects and interests. Such was the pedagogy of Isocrates, who believed that the person who sincerely wishes to speak or write well in order to persuade others will also improve himself in due course.

In all three positions—the Platonist, Aristotelian and Isocratean—rhetoric serves specific functions that bear on the nature and purpose of education as an instrument of social cohesion. Plato, Aristotle, and the sophists were embarked on the search for the answer to a vexing question: can *arete*, or virtue, be taught? Some care is required in considering the point since our term virtue has to be expanded to encompass the many facets of Greek *arete*. Broadly conceived, virtue comprises all those qualities that make for success in society, that secure the admiration of our fellow citizens and that lead to material well-being. The expansiveness of the term is cause enough for disagreements about its nature or the methods for attaining it, and these disagreements underwrite the debate about education. Plato, Aristotle and the sophists read virtue differently, as right conduct or effective action or moral rectitude or some such other idea. They are united, however, in their conception of virtue as the intersection between individual being and social character.

That these three traditions of thought should be similar in the degree to which they each aim to produce virtue, however defined, points up a function of education well established before Plato, Aristotle or the sophists came on the scene. The Greeks, and after them the Romans, drew clear distinctions between liberal and illiberal instruction. True education is not concerned with knowledge that is mechanical or vocational. The trades, technical skills and wage-earning occupations in general were, according to the ancient view, likely to drag down the mind and body. They were therefore unworthy of free men. This sentiment accounts in part for the reliance on slave labor in the ancient world. And it animates the paradox that the birthplace of democracy, Athens, had more slaves than free citizens within its city walls. The notion that true education is somehow occupied with the mind and not the body persists into our time in one form or another. It was a popular notion in antiquity that even some liberal arts, if studied for the wrong reasons or from the wrong principles, could have a similar degrading effect. Education, then, aims at a higher goal. It seeks to produce an individual equipped by history, art and philosophy to live in community with others.

In Plato, the question whether virtue can be taught motivates the Socratic inquiry across a broad front, from the investigation of specific virtues like courage, piety and wisdom, through the analysis of virtue as a concept, to the examination of dialectical reasoning itself as a sort of virtuous activity. In the dialogues named after them, Socrates takes on the great sophists of the day over the question of virtue and its proper pedagogy. He argues with the rhetorician Gorgias about the nature and purpose of rhetoric, with the teacher Protagoras about the nature of virtue and the possibility for its attainment through instruction, and with the polymath Hippias about the nature of knowledge and the mechanisms of comprehension. Plato's Socrates is first allied with then distinguished from the central tenets of sophistic thought. In the *Protagoras*, for example, he ends up defending Protagoras' position that virtue can be taught while Protagoras comes to accept Socrates' assertion that we really do not know what it is.

Socrates and Protagoras are able to arrive at this paradoxical agreement because they both believe, although in radically different terms, that virtue is a form of knowledge. For Socrates, this knowledge is of the eternal *form* of virtue itself. For Protagoras, it is of the social and political *rules* that constrain individuals to act in certain ways. Thus, the two differ over the content of education, but they are allied in the view that education is the key to solving all social and political problems. Each shares a confidence in the belief that if people understand the wrongness of their acts beforehand they would not commit them. Virtuous behavior, whatever its foundation, can be learned. From Socrates' perspective, virtue results from the pursuit of dialectical inquiry into the nature of things and in the habituation to right action. From Protagoras' perspective, virtuous behavior is part of the training that all social beings go through on their way to maturity and civilization. Neither Socrates nor Protagoras would accept the idea that human action is the product of uncontrollable, subconscious, irresistible impulses. To do so would be to admit the impossibility of acting consciously in accord with some concept of virtue.

The educational system that Aristotle describes in the *Politics* ultimately seeks to teach virtue as a prerequisite for the success of the city. That goal requires each citizen, as a thinking being, to develop the correct behavior that sustains himself and his neighbors. He also believes in the power of habituation. It is the root and branch of virtue for Aristotle. In the *Nicomachean Ethics*, where this principle and others are examined, he takes issue with Socrates and Plato.

Knowledge is not the essential component of individual being. Everyday experience proves that men do wrong willingly, often for the most trivial and ignoble reasons. Wrong-doing is not a matter of ignorance. *Character*, much more than either intelligence or knowledge, is the main pillar of the good life. Knowledge is no guarantor of morality. Human beings act as much out of emotion as out of reason. That is why it is important for a person to possess a good disposition, for it inclines him toward the habits of virtuous behavior. Democracy means that the needs of the many will tend to carry the greatest weight in public discussion. The political leader must have what we would call a "cool head" in order to restrain the emotional swing of the majority. After all, as Aristotle points out in his treatise on the subject, politics is not a theory of the ideal city. It concerns the practical administration of an actual city's affairs; it centers on the productive relationship of individuals to each other and to their community. Ethics and politics are interrelated in Aristotle, and education is an important branch of the latter.

Aristotle distinguishes between ethics and politics as distinct practical arts with characteristic means, manners and ends. The virtues of behavior are thus treated one way in ethics, as the subject matter of inquiry, and another way in politics, as the instruments of good government. The dialectic of Plato, however, collapses all such distinctions. Socrates searches for virtue writ large, as the substratum of reality itself. Aristotle divides and analyzes virtue; Plato unites and subsumes it into his Trinity of the Good, the True and the Beautiful. The sophists, however, view virtue as an *operational* quality. It is the mark of good living in the community, whether that be material success, the respect and admiration of friends, or the acquisition of power.

Can virtue be taught? Plato answers no because, ironically, all men share it anyway, and even the pre-eminent among them are clearly unable (like Pericles) to pass that knowledge to their sons. How can we expect lesser souls to do so? Aristotle also answers that virtue cannot be taught since to do so would be merely to teach different systems of virtue, to offer courses in the study of ethics. But it can be learned. A naturally good disposition coupled with positive role models and opportunities to behave virtuously all lead to the habit of virtue. The sophists, though, would claim that virtue can indeed be taught. They would see in Plato's denial an affirmation. The fact that all men share in virtue is proof that it is being taught already. The teaching is done by society. The sophist, a professor of virtue, merely focuses the instruction.

Subsequent reactions to the sophistic pedagogy replicate the intellectual tendencies found in Plato and Aristotle, either investing rhetoric with a characteristic content or setting rhetoric in an informing context of other methods, arts and sciences. Both solutions respond to the perception that sophistic persuasion is groundless, emotional and dangerous. Plato and Aristotle have passed on to us their ethical checks and balances on rhetorical self-consciousness.

The very different notions of rhetoric formulated by Plato, Aristotle and the sophists have been expanded and intertwined in the intervening centuries to produce educational programs that, on the face of it, have very little in common with each other or with us. Yet our own problems in education have their roots in our Graeco-Roman heritage. A history of Western civilization based on the examination of the role played in education by Platonic, Aristotelian and sophistic rhetoric would reveal the periodic emergence of sophistic culture as it is signalled by the dominance of rhetorical assumptions, terms and concepts in public discourse, politics, history, ethics and education. Further, the sophistic epistemology would be shown to exist in the very institution of the school, as an organizing principle of curricula as well as a collection of characteristic teaching methods. And our inquiry would further disclose the existence of sophistic impulses within cultures based upon very different conceptions of thought, expression and action.

The full realization of that project exceeds the present task, but its essential method and direction can be abbreviated for our purpose. The relevance of the approach turns on a simple but trenchant fact. In societies undergoing the sophistic transformation, where the rhetorical commonplaces of present-mindedness and self-confidence hold sway, education becomes the focal point for complex arguments about the proper accommodation of self to community. More often than not, although these arguments are moral, philosophic and cultural, they are always framed by concerns for the relevancy to everyday life of the things being taught in the schools.

Like the Greeks, Roman educators sought to couple moral instruction with practical action. Indeed, Roman sophistication developed out of a yearning to return to traditional Roman virtues set in the context of imperial needs and demands. More so than the Greeks, the Romans were interested in the pragmatic arts of government, both as necessities of rule as well as outlets for personal ambition. The most important theorists of Roman education were Cicero (106–43 B.C.), the Senator and advocate who lived during the final days of the republic, and Quintilian (c. 35–118 A.D.), a professor of rhetoric who taught during the early years of the empire. The span of their lives encompasses the movement of rhetoric in Roman education from an emphasis on vitality and purpose to a preoccupation with performance and technique.

Cicero articulated a philosophy of education that not only addresses what he perceived to be the decline of Roman rectitude, but also aims to produce the man perfectly suited for public service and, by implication, the restoration of Roman values. For him, the ideal Roman conforms to Cato's earlier description of the orator, "a good man skilled in speaking." Cicero, however, greatly sophisticates Cato's definition. Such a man, he argues, needs an art of rhetoric grounded in the knowledge of civic affairs, in the history of Rome, and in the basic principles of philosophy. These are the constituents of pragmatic enlightenment, of knowledge useful to the individual and the community. They constitute the *sine qua non* of Roman culture. "Wisdom without eloquence is seldom helpful," Cicero declares, "and eloquence without wisdom is always dangerous." For him, the educated man is influential because he is articulate.

Quintilian labored under quite different circumstances. Empire brought with it restrictions in the freedom of both speech and action. Oratory, however, still held a high place as a primarily performing art and Quintilian is much more the pedagogue than Cicero. His multi-volume *The Education of an Orator* offers a comprehensive view of Roman education at the time. It begins with elementary education in Book I, the proper content of rhetorical education in Book II, the techniques of rhetoric in Books III–XI and, finally, a theoretical discussion of the higher education (that is, beyond rhetoric) of the orator. The rhetoric Quintilian discusses, however, has become a much narrower and more technical art than Cicero's. And the educational system he devises, while it pays heed to the need to instruct in the cultural values of the Roman culture, lacks the vitality and penetration of Cicero's program to produce the humanistic politician. Quintilian's program serves an empire while Cicero's attempted to revitalize a fading republic. The difference is between a rhetoric that challenges and disturbs and a rhetoric that pleases and reassures.

In the fourth century A.D., St. Augustine appropriated and reformed the rhetoric-centered Roman curriculum of Cicero and Quintilian, with its emphasis on civic virtue and public eloquence, in order to make it suitable for the teaching of Christian piety. Trained in rhetoric and, until he was 32, a professor of the art, Augustine wanted rhetoric to serve not the imperial edict or mundane philosophy but divine revelation. This involved teaching a new way of interpreting God's revealed truth as it is embodied in the Scripture and of reading directly those things which in themselves symbolize his presence in earthly affairs.

Augustine transforms Cicero's rhetoric from a cultural instrument of temporal analysis and articulation to a spiritual tool that deals with eternal truths. He moves beyond, or behind, the mask of language that Cicero accepts as a fact of life, to the substratum of reality that for the Christian mind constitutes the truest expression of God's will. The principles and distinctions of classical rhetoric—Cicero's terminology and the five divisions of his art—are appropriated by Augustine for his *On Christian Doctrine* in order to fit the requirements of persuasion into the setting of the universal truth of Christian doctrine. But Augustine goes even further in his use of ancient rhetorical thought. He develops a rhetorical method by which unchanging truth can be isolated and employed according to the needs of an ever-changing but specifically determined Christian community. Rhetoric becomes in the hands of St. Augustine a tool for inventing the past to fit the requirements of the present. His innovations helped launch an institution, the Catholic Church, which still grounds its pedagogy in the form and content first laid down by him.

In the 12th century, Peter Abailard sought to resolve apparent contradictions between the statements of the Fathers of the Church, the very foundation of both Christian teaching and Church society, by proposing methods of theological analysis he had appropriated from canon law. These methods were essentially comparative and argumentative, for rhetoric survived in one form throughout the Middle Ages as a method of legal analysis. Trained as a dialectician, Abailard understood the power of rhetoric and dialectic to work together as universal arts. In the introduction to 158 contradictory statements by the Church Fathers collected in the *Sic et Non*, he places rhetoric within a hierarchy of methods that reflected and improved upon Aristotle's own ordering of the arts and sciences on the basis of linguistic precision and logical accuracy. His effort would earn him two condemnations for heresy. But the model of his reform, as an intellectual as well as a pedagogical accomplishment, soon gained ground throughout the Christian West and became the basis for scholastic education until the Renaissance.

In the 16th century, Peter Ramus attacked the assumptions of scholastic thought by proposing a new scheme of knowledge that spread Cicero's five divisions of rhetoric—invention, disposition, memory, style and delivery—across the entire curriculum, as the organizing principles for discrete disciplines of study. His separation of logic, language and performance opened the door to subsequent reformers such as Francis Bacon, whose *Organon* sought to systematize all knowledge in discrete sciences, and Rene Descartes, who sought to drive superfluous meaning and rhetorical emotion from the search for the truth. Descartes proposed first to reduce all knowledge to the absolute certainly of his *cogito ergo sum* and then to construct descriptive vocabularies of absolute precision. The Cartesian approach to language, with its emphasis on fixed and precise terminology, lies at the heart of all modern science.

The Enlightenment, the 19th century and the 20th century have produced their own characteristic educational reforms, each of which moves the terms and concepts of rhetoric into novel schemes and epistemologies. As a school subject, rhetoric is making its way back into the curriculum at every level, usually in the guise of courses on "composition" or "public speaking" or "writing across the curriculum." The ebb and flow of its role in education lies at the heart of all disputes about the relevance of education to daily life. It has also animated the various reforms and revolutions, reactions and reestablishments that mark the history of education in Western Culture. For over 2500 years, the debate has been much modified and variously stated. But its content and concerns remain essentially unchanged since it first emerged in the time of Plato, Aristotle and the sophists.

Any educational system tends to encompass paradoxical purposes. It raises questions about virtuous behavior and moral rectitude while, at the same time, it expresses a realistic order and pragmatic function for knowledge. This dichotomy is exaggerated by the emergence of sophistic thinking, which stimulates profound examination of the basic tenets of society itself. Cultural sophistication is a time of upheaval within which education becomes the battleground for all kinds of social, political, moral and aesthetic disputes. Communities in crisis always seem to blame their educators for their distress. Solutions of a wider social nature devised by leaders of one sort or another are often first proposed in relation to the schools. We at once condemn our schools and turn to them for solutions to some present social or moral or political dilemma. Within that context of reformation and revision, the shifting importance of rhetoric gives character to the disputes at hand.

When rhetoric is defined by its techniques and terms, it shrinks to become an art of communication. In the Middle Ages, rhetoric was often identified with preaching or letter-writing or prose composition, the main forms of communication. The sophists who attract the ire of Isocrates, the handbook writers and the eristics, were essentially preoccupied with this reduced form of rhetoric. So too are the modern theorists of communication, who find in rhetoric many useful terms and distinctions for discussing persuasive communication in a variety of fields.

When rhetoric is defined by its content, techniques of argumentative reasoning are made to serve purposes beyond mere argumentation. Rhetoric becomes philosophy, theology, political science, economics or some other such science. For example, Plato's condemnation of rhetoric in the dialogue *Gorgias*, where he continually contrasts it with dialectic, is tempered by his discussion of it in the *Phaedrus*, where he expresses a preference for the life of philosophy over a life of politics and rhetoric. The highest form of rhetoric is actually true philosophy. It is a transformation of rhetoric made by many Platonist thinkers, from St. Augustine to present-day reformers of education.

Contemporary proposals for educational reform often reflect elements of the reductive Platonisms of the past. One of the most controversial, Allan Bloom's *The Closing of the American Mind*, is also the clearest example of the attempt to redirect sophistic education by investing it with a characteristic content. Not that Bloom sees either the problem or his response to it in those terms. Rather, his is a plaint against America's popular culture—the artistic, ethical and technological expression of our sophistication. He stands opposed to the modern sophists, who regard the current turmoil in American culture as indication of the intellectual dynamism, moral freedom and liberated spirit that goes with exploring new realms of human potentiality.

Bloom's solution is an educational program centered on the recognized classical texts of Western thought, the Great Books. Therein, Bloom argues, lie the central truths that constitute true knowledge. Reading these texts imparts the wisdom necessary to halt the decline of American education and reinvigorate a culture consumed with self-gratification, self-assertion and just plain selfishness. For Bloom, as for Plato, educational reform implies substantial moral reformation as well. Bloom's call for a return to a Golden Age when holy texts were interpreted by a priestly class (in this case, university professors) mirrors the Platonist's pining after a republic of ideas ruled by a philosopher-king protected by the guardians of the common wealth. And, like all Platonists, Bloom never bridges the gap between life in the world and the intellectual experiences offered by his selected texts.

Bloom's work exemplifies the central paradox of education. Because education serves so many ends, it has become a political and social battleground. We blame the educational system for the decline in our morality, the slackening of our industrial productivity, the slippage in our ability to compete on a global scale, the erosion of our technological superiority, the ignorance of our citizens and the corruption of politics and business. The public airwaves are thick with contradictory criticisms and suggestions about how we ought to address the present state of our schools. Whatever their merits, these proposals betray deep divisions about the nature and purpose of education in a highly sophisticated society.

On one hand, there are those who think education ought to be primarily concerned with *empowerment*. On the other hand, there are those who feel that education is actually a process of *enlightenment*.

Advocates of empowerment argue that the proper role of education is the transmission of useful information. Utility is the goal of knowledge, in their view. The schools are training centers for a work force that needs to be adequately equipped to meet the challenges of economic competition in the post-Cold War world. Empowerment requires a curriculum that stresses "practical" skills such as reading, writing and mathematics. The advocates of empowerment tend to be concerned with such concepts as "subject matter," "relevance," "adaptation" and "product." After all, the exercise of power—personal, professional or national—requires a defined epistemology of action and production. It is concerned more with the fundamental questions "what do we know" and "how do we communicate (or employ) what we know" than with "how do we know that we know." The latter smacks of metaphysical uncertainty and logic-chopping. Empowerment, though, deals with concrete possibilities.

Advocates of enlightenment, however, argue that the schools ought to transmit edifying cultural values and essential principles of civilized conduct. Virtue is the goal of knowledge. Education's major purpose is to produce a citizenry cognizant of its moral obligations to the home, the family and the nation. Advocates of enlightenment focus on the epistemological question, "how do we know that we know anything at all?" Enlightenment entails coming to terms with the few principles and assumptions that animate systems of thought and organize systems of community and government. Thought is higher than action, in their scheme of things, although "correct" conduct is the ultimate product of the enlightened mind. Enlightenment requires a curriculum that stresses literature, philosophy, history, and perhaps religion because these are the fountain heads of a culture defined by its intellectual, moral and artistic products. Advocates of enlightenment tend to be concerned with such concepts as "authority," "doctrine," and "values" since these entail the thorough understanding of the basis of proper behavior.

The moral certitude that derives from enlightenment is also a kind of empowerment since it liberates the mind from the petty tyrannies of ignorance through self-knowledge, self-assertion and self-defense. Likewise, the informed, empowered mind is the only true foundation for moral character since morality itself must be established actively and energetically in a world of competing values. In practice, however, these two positions are essentially contradictory. They mandate distinctly different educational methods and structures as well as different ends. In plain terms, the choice is often posed between vocational education (or job and, more recently, professional training) on the one hand and liberal education (or value training) on the other. A great deal of time and money is spent at all levels of the American education establishment to meet these differing objectives and, in a few instances, to marry them.

Yet the current debate about education does not take into account a relatively recent transformation of American culture that affects not only education but also the broader relationship between individual being and social character in a democracy. This transformation is powered by high-technology instruments of mass communication—computers, satellites and the like—and it is informed by the techniques of advertising and public relations. It encompasses the way we communicate with each other and with our neighbors in the world. It also controls how we regard ourselves, as independent individuals in a world community increasingly marked by interdependence.

The revolution in technologies of communication inevitably affects the epistemological concerns about the nature and use of knowledge. It also transforms the connections between knowing and doing, thought and action, theory and practice, for empowerment and enlightenment share a common aspect in America. They both seek to produce within the individual the *capacity for action* albeit in different senses of the verb "to act." Empowerment concerns doing, creating or making, or acting upon something external to ourselves. It is controlled by certain economic or productive constraints. The empowered individual is capable of *efficient action*. Enlightenment concerns behaving in accord with internalized values. It is controlled by social or cultural or religious constraints. The enlightened individual is capable of *right-minded action*. The debate about education is paradoxical in the degree to which it envisions efficient and right-minded action as opposed; that is, the extent to which it regards theory and practice as distinctly different pursuits.

Education for efficient action benefits primarily the individual by making it possible for him to work for some profitable end. It is self-rewarding. Education for right-minded action benefits the community at large by assuring that as individuals pursue their own ends, they are ever mindful of the need to preserve the common wealth. It is socially rewarding. But empowerment and enlightenment are only two facets of the three-fold phenomenon we call education. In a culture that is built on confidence in the power of words and the reality of images and is rooted in the belief that change is inevitable and truth is relative, education has also come to assume another more vital and influential purpose. Education so conceived produces neither empowerment nor enlightenment. Like the other concepts of education, this third alternative also aims to teach us how "to act," but in the dramatic sense of the word, as the skillful portrayal of thoughts and emotions through *pretense* and *imitation*. Its end is public performance or *enactment*.

Education for enactment deals ultimately with the capacity for *affective action*, the influencing of other people through emotional appeals. It goes well beyond the elementary courses in persuasive writing or public speaking that most schools now offer. These are merely fragments of an epistemology of affectation that has the potential to organize the entire curriculum of study. In fact, the formal institutions of learning do a poor job of teaching pretense and imitation, the chief components of an education dedicated to enactment. More likely than not, the student learns these skills accidentally, by manipulating his teachers in order to earn a better grade and by navigating grading systems, curricula and programs of study for personal ends.

In the sophisticated culture of America, pretense and imitation are cultivated in the marketplace, the public forum, the workplace, the street, the social gathering and in the arts, wherever individuals negotiate success and failure in a democratic environment under the influence of competing assertions about reality advanced by other members of the community. Things are rarely as they seem to be in a world that is increasingly defined by the mass communication of emotive words and evocative images. Not only survival but prosperity as well depends on the ability to discern the difference between what people think, what they say and what they do. It is this disruption of thought, expression and action that confronts the sensitive mind on a daily basis with the duplicities of modern life. Moving from conception to enactment requires a special knowledge that is rarely taught in the schools. That is why a new educational industry has sprung up in America, privately funded and operating outside the realm of the institutions of formal, or "official," education. In form and content this new industry is the contemporary expression of the ancient sophistic programs of self-improvement and self-assertion. It exploits a flaw in modern technological education. Instead of fostering a general appreciation for diversity and the utility of the humane arts of living well, our educational institutions reward narrowness and parochialism. They lead us away from the integrated life and demand instead that we specialize our interests and declare our intentions before we even know them. The result is a pervasive inarticulateness compounded by unhappiness, impotence and confusion.

Now, however, it is possible to enroll in privately-sponsored courses that promise to help overcome the disabilities of formal education. These purport to make it possible for you to succeed in business, or to gain confidence in public settings or to be satisfied in personal relations. Numerous institutes are dedicated to theories and systems of thought that embody our confidence in language, our trust in images, our belief in change and our conviction that the truth is what we make it. They rival the traditional establishments of higher learning for the attention of decision-makers in industry and government because they promise a program with pragmatic results, one that improves the image of the organization, inspires its leadership, or increases employee satisfaction and productivity. The proponents of pretense and imitation are primarily responsible for providing American society with its leaders and opinion-makers.

Education in America is thus concerned with "learning to act" in three senses: learning to do, learning to behave, and learning to pretend. And the new sophists of education fuse the goals of empowerment and enlightenment into programs that aim at the advancement of the individual within some larger social setting: the workplace, the political arena, the profession, even the family. They declare openly what most of us feel in our hearts, that merit and knowledge and good intentions alone will not win the competition for recognition, promotion and self-realization. On the one hand, they promise to fulfill the goal of empowerment by enabling each person to compete in a fluid, dynamic, unpredictable universe. On the other hand, they promise to fulfill the goal of enlightenment by equipping each person with the commonplace values and virtues necessary to understanding success in contemporary sophistic culture. In both instances, they treat the challenges of everyday life in an ever-changing world as essentially *semantic*, to be addressed incompletely but usefully by means of a new science of provocative symbolism. Whatever their specific differences in method or terminology, the modern sophists all teach the facile manipulation of pretense and imitation. Ultimately, the advocates of sophistic learning claim to resolve the paradox of education, the contradiction between empowerment and enlightenment, by making theory and practice one and the same thing. Success is its own proof of validity in the calculus of affectation.

Because sophistic culture is increasingly defined around appearances, pretense and imitation have assumed a central position in every sphere of interaction. They are the fabric of life itself in a country where pragmatism is equated with "whatever works." They shape how we come to know ourselves and each other. They control how we judge the character of causes and the consequences of action. And they determine how we come to terms with other peoples and cultures. No matter its form or content, all education aims to bring the individual mind into some accommodation with its physical, social, and spiritual surroundings. As psychological capacities and social phenomena, pretense and imitation are central to the pedagogy of sophistic culture. They are the intermediaries between individual being and social character and, as such, affect the ethical as well as the historical, political, educational and aesthetic aspects of the sophisticated life.

CHAPTER FIVE

Seeking the Self:
The Plight of
Sophisticated Ethics

*No sooner do men despair of living forever than they are
disposed to act as though they are to exist but for a single day.*
—Alexis de Tocqueville

A civilization may be characterized by its conception of virtue.
—Will Durant

THE GREEKS DEFINED YET ANOTHER realm of inquiry in their quest to understand the human mind at work in its social setting. They recognized that history, politics and education all presume characteristic relationships between thought and action, intention and result, statement and deed, appearance and reality, the one and the many. Each relationship possesses a unique *ethos*, or character, that simultaneously grows out of, reflects back upon and subsequently determines the quality of life for the thinking being. This systematic reflection on motives and ends is called *ethics*, and it produces schema for the organization of all human interactions, from the musings of the individual to the manipulations between human beings and the manifold operations of society.

Whatever superficial complexities characterize the study of ethics, the search for connections between thought, action and expression oscillates between the desire to discover the comprehensive nature of all human society and the demand for comprehensible rules and standards of personal conduct. Conscientiously erected ethical systems are concerned with identifying and isolating the fundamental constituent of *being* that gives character to action, pattern to behavior, sense to belief and system to community.

Action, behavior, belief and community are the social coordinates of self-knowledge and self-control. The realization of the self always occurs in the context of others, amid the hubbub and confusion of life in society. Whatever special term we put to self-realization—individuation, individualization, separation, independence, cognition, or consciousness—the dialogue between individual being and social character eventually leads to the emergence of the one among the many. Education, as we have seen, attempts in some way to foster that emergence by strengthening the bonds between individuality and social purpose. But our confusion over the nature and purpose of education is mirrored and amplified in our uncertainty about the nature and end of ethics.

It is no accident that there is much discussion of ethics lately. Cultures in the midst of the sophistic transformation are plagued with concerns about morality and rightness. The Greeks were early explorers of this territory and their innovations and discoveries set the terms of our present quandary. The rise of sophistic thinking in the fifth century B.C. sparked a debate that still rages today, although the vocabulary of ethics has become complex and specialized indeed. Ethics took shape in the years between the birth of Socrates and the death of Aristotle when Greek thinkers grappled with the problems of conduct in society. Socrates spent his life inquiring after the foundations of virtue. The sophists divined that power itself is the supreme authority in a relativist universe, and they devoted themselves to teaching others how to employ that simple notion for personal gain in the public sphere. Plato dedicated several dialogues to the exploration of ethical behavior and right reason, showing in the process both the indeterminacy of dialectical investigation and the linkage between intelligent inquiry and virtue. Aristotle elaborated the first scientific treatment of ethics as a special branch of knowledge in the hope that understanding would flow from analysis. The search for virtue, the nature and uses of power, the role of inquiry in coming to consciousness and the rationalization of morality are still favorite themes of ethicists.

We, too, are preoccupied with the calculus of individual behavior and social action. Television talk shows are crowded with experts of all persuasions commenting on the perceived decline in the morality of our children, our public servants, our leaders, our politicians and our artists. Despite the apparent profusion of notions about ethics, some of which are intricately constructed, it has come to be identified simply with "legality." Rarely does it encompass our private affairs, that is, those which do not involve some aspect of the public interest or the public trust. This narrowing of our common sense of ethics allows us to address the problems that crop up between individual being and social character, between private desires and public good, in a manner that reflects the pragmatic nature of our own sophistic culture.

When we are confronted with a problem of ethics, we follow a characteristic course of action. Committees are impaneled to investigate the causes of unethical behavior and to establish standards of conduct to guide a variety of personal and professional activities in the future. Our political, commercial and educational leaders inveigh against cheating and other forms of bad dealing. They empower departments of ethics to enforce newly devised standards of public conduct. Prominent people who hold the public trust publicly swear allegiance to right action. Other prominent people who have been branded as unethical are brought to account for their behavior, usually in the law courts, before congressional investigating committees, or some such other open forum that operates in at least a quasi-judicial fashion. Educators rush to teach classes in ethics though these generally tend to be surveys of the various ethical systems that have emerged in Western civilization at one time or another. The news media focus on the crimes and punishments of wrong-doers. The entertainment industry produces a movie or a docudrama celebrating the trials and triumphs of an individual who heroically confronted and resolved an ethical dilemma. Government and business make a show of protecting "whistle-blowers," self-appointed guardians of ethical behavior, and the news media lionize them.

When all is said and done, the ruling institutions of government, commerce and education present the rest of us with finely crafted, ornately composed, aesthetically pleasing considerations of the perceived deficiencies and possible remedies of human nature. Ethics is defined as a lack of malfeasance, and proper behavior, as that which avoids even the *appearance* of wrong-doing.

Still, there is an explanation to be made for why we are presently consumed by ethics and, also, why our preoccupation has come to nothing. Of all the indications that sophistic thinking has triumphed in the 20th century, none is more telling than the death of ethics—not the ethics of the popular media, of the show trials and staged recantations, but ethics as a concept of individual being and self-worth. Ours is a time not only of great turmoil and change, but also of selfishness and egotism. Self-interest has become the central principle of communal life. The paradox of that proposition bedevils our search for common grounds of action. Ethics requires a clear, unflinching perception of things *as they are* as well as an ironclad dedication to the pursuit of the truth. It is the rawest form of mindfulness. Now, however, selective amnesia controls our search for the truth about our selves as well as each other. Fixed standards of conduct and commonly accepted notions of fairness and fair play find no home either as ethical principles or as foundations of intellectual inquiry. Like shady accountants who bilk their employers a dollar at a time, we balance the books to suit our own immediate goals. In a culture dedicated to "management by objective," the ends do indeed justify the means.

Our ethical dilemma—the absence of any concept of ethics as something other than a serviceable legalism (which is actually an elaborate contingent verisimilitude)—arises from the five commonplaces of sophistic culture. Information is power. Words are tools. Images are real. Change is inevitable. Truth is relative. These are not only the essential criteria for knowledge and action, they also condition how we conceive of our selves and how we treat each other. They control, that is, the evolving relationship between individual being and social character.

When information is power, power flows and shifts according to standards of usage which are themselves arbitrary, transient and oblique. Information no longer produces a *state of being*, what we call "knowledge." It is constantly in a *state of perpetual change*, of becoming something else. Information is a commodity, like soy beans, pork bellies and oil, to be bartered on the open market. It is always traded against its future worth. Consequently, information rarely possesses intrinsic value; it only "informs" in context. "To be informed" once meant "to know." Now, it simply means "to be capable of doing" something for an intelligible and immediate end. We have radicalized the already terse response of the sophistic epistemology to the ancient questions of knowledge: What do we know? How do we know that we know? How do we tell what we know? Simply put, information is power because we need only know that which we must communicate for some purpose. All else is meaningless noise until such time as it becomes appropriate. *Relevancy* is a central principle of thought and action in our times. Its ascendancy has signalled the death of history, as an intellectual concept as well as an academic subject. For the past is but another category of information, an invention that is important only when it serves some purposeful present-mindedness.

Since communication is both the cause and effect of power, words are valued for their utility. Language is regarded as an instrument of symbolic action to be wielded mindfully and efficiently, in the context of immediate effectiveness. We have expanded the categories of symbols that constitute language and multiplied the vehicles for their communication. Each person now must know many languages in order to negotiate the passage of a day. Some are technical, others colloquial, yet others specific to particular times or places or circumstances. Only when spoken language can be pared down to some essential emotive quality or persuasive character is it seen as useful. We spend most of our time trapped in an enduring irony, arguing in often imprecise terms about the meanings and intentions behind the words we use. Lawyers, psychologists and public relations experts are now the high priests of linguistic interpretation. Intentionality and motive have assumed a central position in the public use of language. Most people, however, would prefer not to think too long about words and their ambiguities. They only confuse and confound the search for meaning amid the sophisticated noise of daily life. Still, there is no avoiding completely the entanglement of words. That is why *literacy*, conceived of as the most basic capacity for understanding and communicating useful information, has become the goal of those who purport to promote the effective use of language. But literacy so defined reduces our appreciation for the power of words and, more telling, misrepresents the role language plays in daily life. The adoption of literacy as a utilitarian skill rather than as a liberating exercise of informed consciousness signals the death of poetry as a mode of perception as well as expression.

The perceiving mind is more likely to be schooled in the rhetoric of visual images, in the expressions of form rather than the figures of speech. To generations reared on television and cinema, images are real. They indicate a vital presence beyond spoken language. They are felt before they are explained, experienced before they are understood. We are tongue-tied when it comes to describing the images that affect us, whether they are generated in advertising, politics or art. The realms of communal action are now bound together by their dependence on imagistic communication. *Visibility*, conceived as sharpness or distinctness or clarity or prominence, has become the central concept of art and life in a world controlled by the commonplaces of rhetoric. Its centrality signals the death of reasoned discourse formulated in syllogisms and expressed in words as the basis for certainty as well as change.

Change is the only certainty. Self-confidence is now based on the assumption that things are never as they seem to be, nor do they remain as they are for very long. Our reality is built on shifting notions of improvement, progress, alteration, adaptation and accommodation. Change is inevitable in a culture powered by technological innovation, founded on materialism and dedicated to the fulfillment of individual desires and potencies. The recognition that change, not stability, controls daily life has led to the psychology of personal growth. The human *being*, long regarded as a finished product of some sort of divine creation, has been replaced by the human *becoming*, a flawed entity demanding self-improvement, if not perfection. The inevitability of change has not only destabilized the long-standing relationship between humanity and God or humans and Nature, it has also altered the potential for intimacy between people and the possibility for self-knowledge. *Instability* is the ruling principle of a universe perceived as tending towards chaos. Its fundamental role in the unfolding of both the natural and artificial worlds signals the death of mythology as the primary archetype guiding social action as well as individual development.

All societies confront the paradoxes generated when individuals attempt to balance their own well-being against the demands of social character. Sophistic cultures face the added burden of deciding, at any moment, what constitutes the norms of behavior best suited for the simultaneous attainment of personal happiness and public efficiency. The enduring myths, which in other circumstances have assumed a theological importance as indicators of proper behavior in the presence of blind fate or the interfering gods, have been replaced by the often trivial contingent verisimilitudes of daily life. The hold of verisimilitude over our dealings with one another acquires a semblance of durability from the conventions and practices of law. But law is ultimately only a shared confidence in the arrangements between us and, like all confidence, it can be destroyed by betrayal, duplicity and misrepresentation. The strength of contracts lies in the willing participation of the parties to them. The resort to law is itself a sophisticated contingent verisimilitude. In such a circumstance the truth, especially when it is defined by the prescriptions of law, is relative to many things: statement, proof, belief, interpretation, expectation, speculation, the past, the present, fact and fiction. It exists only when it can be agreed upon, and then only according to the warrants of necessity and the capacity for belief. *Relativity* is the dominant concept of a culture based on the dialectic between the opinions of the many and the prejudices of the few or the one. Its power over the relationships between people as well as its control of the judgments of the individual mind signals the triumph of legalism and the death of morality or, in broader terms, the victory of the fitting or the appropriate over the universally true.

Relevancy, literacy, visibility, instability and relativity are the basis of the so-called *situational ethics* that are at the heart of the pervasive legalism of sophistic culture. Law is built on distinctions between deeds and consequences. It is everywhere concerned with the circumstances of action and the formation of intent. The concept of *opportunity* formulated by Gorgias in the fifth century B.C. has become in the 20th century A.D. the fundamental basis of legal reasoning. *Timeliness* frames the on-going dialogue between private interest and public good.

The moral relativism of situational ethics is applied by way of language. The invention of linguistic distinctions precedes the invention of moral or ethical or legal distinctions. These are always applied dialectically—as oppositions between good and evil, right and wrong, useful and useless, the one and the many, the real and the apparent, the true and the false—in words, that is, with values already attached to them. Consequently, the dialectical analysis of terms is conducted within the confines of rhetorical purposefulness. It rarely leads to synthesis, the construction of new, subsuming terminologies and concepts. Rather, the dialectic of ethical debate is constructed around clearly marked stances. This is most evident with respect to issues such as abortion and euthanasia, where the argument has been pushed to its extremes, the choice between individual rights and the social good. In all such instances, the dialectical underpinning of relativism is meant to vivify differences and discord rather than to clarify similarities and concordance.

But the questions that lie behind every dilemma involving individual being and social character remain largely unexamined in our time except perhaps by a few isolated specialists in academia. They certainly do not figure into the consideration of actual cases. They lurk, however, on the periphery of our consciousness, poking through here and there when the discussion of right and wrong action touches upon compelling causes. These questions are ancient in origin, for they were first asked in Athens over 2500 years ago by philosophers, sophists and poets. What is the "good life?" Is it measured by wealth or power or popularity? Or does it entail a private, internal quality, an intellectual sense as well as an external expression? Are material success and personal integrity mutually exclusive? Can the needs of individual being be brought into accord with the demands of social harmony?

These questions go beyond merely searching for the standards of right and wrong *action* to call into view the true and false *assumptions* that guide our daily dealings with one another and support our basic beliefs about the way human beings ought to live together. They encompass, that is, the obligations that bind individuals to one another within specific communities. Moreover, these communities can be defined in a variety of ways, either as geographical entities or as collections of like-minded individuals pursuing similar interests. However conceived, in whatever communal context, the ancient questions about the good life pivot on the intricate nature of selfhood. As the Greeks first recognized, self-discipline, self-control and self-respect are components not only of individual integrity but also of communal strength. Yet we pay lip service to these qualities of character. They do not fit into the system of rewards that we have established for those who are to be judged successful. Self-discipline, self-control and self-respect are breaking down completely, owing to great confusion about the relationship between individual being and social character—between the pursuit of individual happiness and the maintenance of the common good. We have no clear view either of virtue or of how best to attain it.

The history of ethics is shaped by disagreements over the nature of virtue—whether it can be known and taught, whether it is central or peripheral to social progress, whether it is a form of knowledge or a kind of power, whether it exists either as an ideal of individual being or as an empirical part of social organization. Viewed in terms of the struggle to locate virtue amid the flux and flow of communal life, Thucydides' vast history of the

Peloponnesian War becomes something more than the story of political conflict. It also encompasses the cultural struggle of the age as well. His contrasting of the Athenian and Spartan characters is framed by the different value each places on the individual. The fifth century B.C., which ended in the cataclysm of Thucydides' war, saw the emergence for the first time in Western history of the opposition between individual prerogatives and social compulsions. That opposition was thorough, penetrating and transforming, a truly revolutionary episode in the development of self-consciousness in the West. It was propelled by the emerging social theories of the sophists which valued individuality over communal traditions. As a result of their efforts, man-made law supplanted mythic tradition as the basis for social peace and progress.

The dialectical tension of the age finds its clearest expression in Plato, whose Socratic dialogues examine specific virtues—courage, piety, wisdom, temperance—against the background of collaborative action in the *polis*. Plato was no friend of democracy or individual rights, at least as we have come to understand them. He regarded the democratic organization of the state to be at best inefficient and, more likely, downright disruptive and dangerous. His solution, as we have seen by the idealization of the *polis* in his *Politeia*, emphasizes the hierarchical ordering of society. Those who are most capable of statecraft lead the rest of the *polis* by the example of their lives and their skill with dialectic.

The necessity for leadership of merit and birth acquires an epistemology of sorts in the *Protagoras*, where virtue can be known only in its parts, by its particular manifestations in specific circumstances. Such knowledge is incomplete, but when viewed through the lens of dialectical inquiry it is suggestive of the larger sense of virtue. For Plato, virtue as an *idea* is greater than the sum of its manifested parts, the many instances of behavior that we would call virtuous. Indeed, it must be so, since people will often disagree about virtue in the specific instance only to find grounds for agreement about it in the abstract. For Protagoras, virtue is a form of power, the intelligent influence over other minds through the affectations of persuasion and the mechanisms of politics. It is embodied in the ability to engage effective public behavior within the constraints of culture and community. Thus, while Plato sees virtue as timeless, unchanging, and immutable, the sophist argues that it is everywhere timely, circumstantial and evolutionary. Since man is the measure of all things in Protagorean thought, virtue itself is measurable by an assessment of its effects on the operations of society. It can be observed in action everyday, in the marketplace and the meeting halls of the *polis* and, more important, it can be transmitted to the young by instruction and by example.

These two conceptions of virtue—as a unitary, eternal ideal and as a fragmentary, temporal reality—are the poles between which ethical systems are strung. Both underwrite pragmatic concepts of informed action. The unitary, eternal ideal is the basis of all religion, while the fragmentary, temporal reality is the basis of all politics. Behavior in the first case is measured against interpretations of unchanging principles and, in the second, against changing standards of effective action. Clearly, all societies are mixtures of the two since the dialectic between skepticism and sophistry, the basic psychological impulses of the ideal and the real that one finds in Plato's *Protagoras*, figures prominently in the operation of real communities. Put another way, human organizations waver between self-confidence and self-doubt, between beliefs assumed to be true and opinions assumed to be false. It is the role of the well-ordered state, according to both Plato and the sophists, to provide the mechanisms by which truth and falsity can be known in order to warrant the common actions of individuals pursuing different goals.

The innovations of sophistic thought played hard against the commonly accepted conceptions of orderly society that had supported the emergence of Athens as a power among the Greeks. The deterioration of that culture provides the dramatic setting for Plato's dialogues much as it forms the subject matter for Thucydides' cataclysmic history. In the *Protagoras*, Plato has Socrates and Protagoras seek the basis of moral reality within the flux of human history and politics. Socrates inclines toward the eternal and Protagoras toward the temporal, but both see virtue as emerging somehow in the context of community. At its most essential level, Plato's *Protagoras* treats the dialectic of individual being and social character as the driving force behind the formation, maintenance and even perfection of the *polis*. The dialectical interplay between individuality and social cohesion is the fundamental unit of ethics.

The sophists are the cultural representatives of individualism, as an idea and as a way of life. They appear on the scene in the first place in response to a demand for higher education on the part of the young men of the leisure class, Plato's class. They are confident proponents of the power of the imagination, and they teach a program of self-improvement and self-assertion that bedevils those who pine after a more stable, predictable and ultimately controllable social organization. To them, virtue consists in the efficient performance of whatever one sets out to do. It certainly does not inhere in the blind obedience to largely unquestioned rules and customs. Tradition is their enemy, innovation their creed, "question authority" their motto. Law, according to them, ought to widen the possibilities of individual development, not constrict them either to heredity or to artificial, social distinctions. Moreover, there is a law higher than those found in the codes of the state, and superior to them as well. It is a natural law that resides in the heart of every man, thus making us all potential judges of right and wrong. The conscience of the individual is above the dictates of any state.

Plato, of course, was alarmed by these innovations. And he greatly sophisticates Socrates' impulse toward the eternal and unchanging ideal in response to them. His conception of virtue places it at the core of reality, not simply as a descriptive term for laudable action, but as a prescriptive concept ruling right-mindedness in all its incarnations, as history, politics, education and art. It exists beyond the reach of mere law and certainly beyond the grasp of the mind unaided by dialectic. Plato sees in the sophistic ethic a direct threat to the discovery and development of the superior being, the person of clearly compelling intelligence and command who by virtue of his intellectual powers deserves to lead the state. Despite Plato's victory over the sophists in the scholarly tradition of Western ideas,

Protagoras' view, not Plato's, accords more closely to our own concept of reality, and not just because we are somehow the victims of an elaborate sophistic conspiracy. Plato's ideal state, after all, remains a dream never intended for enactment on earth. It serves as the model for the relationship between individual being and social character that Plato considers the only real salvation for the troubled mind of the sophisticated self. Protagoras' own creation myth, relayed by Plato in the dialogue bearing the sophist's name, encapsulates the theme of progress that has shaped Western civilization ever since. We are heirs to a twofold tradition: the sophistic vision of society made good through self-conscious effort and the platonic fear of society gone bad through self-conscious deceit.

Aristotle was the first to introduce *ethic* as a technical term, to describe a wholly formed, independently defined field of inquiry. In this he differs markedly from his predecessors. Plato is everywhere concerned with the ethical, although he nowhere describes a system of ethics in detail or, for that matter, with much coherence. On the other hand, the sophists trivialize ethical concerns by making them coordinates of power and persuasion. For Aristotle, however, ethics is but one discipline of human knowledge. It is closely related, on one hand, to politics, since it entails some aspect of pursuing the good in collaboration with others, and on the other, to rhetoric, since it also concerns what moves men to action. The distinction of ethics as a separate field of inquiry is important to Aristotle; he clearly sees himself as an innovator in this respect. According to Aristotle, his predecessors lacked a certain refinement in their analyses of ethics. Plato and the sophists contribute to the discussion, to be sure, but they left it undeveloped. They focused, Aristotle alleges, too narrowly on virtue and lost sight of the true subject matter of ethics. Virtue is praiseworthy and it is essential to a clear understanding of the science of ethics, but it is not the end of the subject. In this Aristotle is realistically simple, for the aim of life is not goodness, but happiness. Consequently, it is necessary to understand both the nature of the good and, ultimately, how happiness derives from its attainment.

The peculiar excellence of man is his power of thought. It

alone allows him to surpass and rule the other creatures of the world. Aristotle presumes that happiness lies in the full functioning of this specifically human quality. Thus, the chief condition of happiness is the life of reason. Virtue, or more accurately *excellence* (since the Greek *arete* carries more meaning than the term virtue can bear), depends on clear judgment, self-control and balanced desires. Moreover, the path to *arete* follows the middle way, or the golden mean. Every quality of character that Plato investigates in his dialogues, for example, can be arranged in a triad, with the first and last qualities being the extremes, or vices, and the middle quality a virtue, or excellence. Between cowardice and rashness lies courage, between humility and pride is modesty, between quarrelsomeness and flattery, friendship, and so on with all the traits of character.

The "right" in ethics is not much different from "rightness" in mathematics or engineering, according to Aristotle. It denotes the fitting or appropriate, what works to the best result. The golden mean is not a mathematical mean, however, the average of two calculable extremes. On the contrary, it fluctuates according to the enveloping circumstances of each situation. Consequently, ethics is not a science as precise as mathematics, for it must admit to the indeterminacies of human nature and the ambiguities of human circumstance. And it can be revealed only to the mature intellect. *Arete* is the product of art, it is the result of practice and habituation. It does not reside in the act, but in the habit of mind that is built up through the exercise of virtuous action.

Aristotle's formulation of the golden mean reflects a characteristic attitude among the Greeks. Plato had it in mind when he called virtue "harmonious action." Aristotle's approach is markedly different from Plato's, however, where dialectical analysis is intended to produce an understanding of virtue itself. Aristotle's position also differs from that of the sophists, where virtue is the product of successful action. In many respects, Aristotle's vision of ethics combines the idealistic elements of Plato with the pragmatic concerns of the sophists. The golden mean is meant to balance the impulsive desires of the individual being seeking itself against the communal requirements of the wholly activated social character. Happiness, for Aristotle, is a pleasure of the mind, and it can only be trusted when it comes from the pursuit or the capture of the truth.

These different philosophic conceptions of virtue and right action may find expression in our own discussions of ethics, but merely as verbal vestiges of a reality that no longer holds true. For our peculiar sophistication amplifies and transforms the essential philosophic dialogue among Plato, the sophists and Aristotle over the relationship of individual to community, the citizen to his *polis*. The Platonists among us argue for standards of conduct related to transcendental values. The clearest proponents are the fundamentalists in religion and politics who, in different terms and for different ends, urge a return to immutable values, the restitution of official morality and rigorous enforcement of the written codes of human behavior. The modern sophist, when he thinks at all about ethics, usually endorses an attitude about behavior that values success in life as the proof of ethical worthiness. The modern Aristotelian, on the other hand, does not talk much about the golden mean. That is the stuff of Sunday school. Rather, he makes distinctions and works out definitions to express a gradation of action that at any point can be assessed according to its mix of rightness and wrongness.

All contemporary thinkers reduce ethics to a discussion about means and ends but in a manner quite different from that which animated the ancient moral calculus. Plato, the sophists and Aristotle proposed solutions, albeit radically different ones, to specific problems of community and self-knowledge. They *invented*, that is, arguments or systems or disciplines in response to the analysis of the circumstances at hand. After all, the rise of sophistication among the Greeks involved the application of power in fulfillment of private or public desires. But we proceed from a concept of invention that reverses the direction of analysis. The plague of drugs, for example, is treated as a police or military problem, and we resort to preexisting "solutions," in this case the established mechanisms of police and military power. We define the issue in terms of law enforcement and the punishment of criminal behavior rather than according to some other model of behavior, a medical or social or economic one, because the means of enforcement already exist. The means dictate the end although we argue passionately and with conviction that the reverse is true. Indeed, the "means" are simply circumstances within which it is possible to invent problems that accommodate solutions already known to exist.

This inversion of the traditional rhetorical notion of invention bears on the most important aspects of individual being and social character. For ethical considerations entail a psychology of the self. Greek sophistic thinkers stimulated the initial movement toward self-consciousness in Western Culture. The issues they raised fueled the reaction of Plato and the accommodation of Aristotle to sophistic thought in general. The Greeks were concerned with the realization of the self, variously defined as the soul or the citizen or the social actor. Because they placed man in the context of other men, individuals in communities, they also realized that self-expression was of paramount importance in the search for self-consciousness and self-knowledge. That is one reason why Plato, the sophists and Aristotle sought either the accommodation with or the destruction of rhetoric as an art, an attitude and a mode of perception. It alone among the humane arts fully embodies both the frailties and the potentialities of human nature. It alone envisions power as the product of the active mind acting on others through language. The awareness of one's self in context, sophisticated self-consciousness, is at the heart of all conceptions of rhetoric.

For Plato, self-consciousness is the product of dialectical inquiry into the nature of the good, the true and the beautiful. It is a kind of harmony between the self and the eternal ideas of which life in the world is only a pale imitation. By reaching for a more fundamental understanding of why things are as they seem to be, the mind comes to see itself for what it is. Plato rejects rhetorical self-consciousness as an illusion that stands in the way of true knowledge. It treats *becoming*, not *being*. Instead of bringing the mind to awareness of itself, rhetoric merely arms the user with the weapons of self-justification and self-delusion. It deals only with life's verisimilitudes, not with the compelling reality of the Ideas.

For Aristotle, self-consciousness entails the use of all the arts and sciences to analyze the causes and effects of action. Aristotle's rhetorician is self-conscious about several things: the nature of his art, the premises of his argument, the kinds of speeches and audiences, his own character and purpose. He also understands the effects of rhetorical speech and assumes responsibility for final consequences. Aristotle accommodates rhetorical self-consciousness in the larger scheme of the arts and sciences, as a way of thinking about common opinions and beliefs. Verisimilitude is an essential part of reality, for it haunts not only art and literature but politics, rhetoric and ethics as well.

The sophist, however, teaches another kind of self-consciousness. It is an awareness of the potential for representation in all kinds of situations. The search for self is misplaced, the sophist would argue, if it seeks a unitary being or single animating soul. We are all a collection of many "selves," each with a purpose dictated by the external circumstances of its creation and employment. The sophist traffics in what the Greeks would call *ecstasy*, a reveling in the temporary derangements of personal being. He teaches how to become *beside* yourself at the opportune time in order to gain some end, perform some function, enact some character. Man is an actor who writes his own role in the unfolding drama of life. Virtue and the good are not external qualities to be discovered through circumventing logic or dialectical exercise. They reside in the power of the mind to create its contingent verisimilitudes, to set the world dancing to its tune. The sophist always prefers *epideixis*, public display, to *dialexis*, inquiry by question and answer. For it is only in performance, the sophist would argue, that you can truly realize your abundant selves. Sophistry is at heart an acting profession, filled with presumption, pretense and representation. The sophistic self is always located outside the individual, in the circumstances that dictate—and the contingent verisimilitudes that manifest—rhetorical self-consciousness.

Sophistic thought is peculiarly suited to our time because we have lost confidence in fundamental concepts of decency and respect, in our power to govern ourselves, in moral principles, in personal responsibility and in the whole foundation of communal existence. Ours is an age adrift, and like the Golden Age of Greece is constructed on confusion and crisis. Rhetorical self-consciousness has always come to the fore when tradition loses its power over thought and action. The ministry of self-improvement that the sophists offered the Athenians was tied intimately to the emergence of individuality in the scheme of social and political power. Persuasion occurs not only in the formal context of systems, institutions and mechanisms of government. It grows out of the projection of personality and character, of *ethos* as the Greeks understood it. Such were the conditions of Athens in the fifth century B.C. Such are the realities of American life on the cusp of the 21st century. Pretense and imitation assume a central role in the definition of the self when sophistication becomes the primary arbiter of right and wrong. *Seeming to be* is *being itself* in a community controlled by relativity, opportunity and probability.

Consequently, sophistic culture inclines toward chaos and disarray. The democratization of power, the assertion of equity over justice, the empowerment of individuals in their own sovereignty, the choice of means over ends, the primacy of action over thought, the preference for becoming over being—all these tendencies assure that ethical standards of a universal nature are impossible to devise. Sophistication is a process of becoming that only seems to be a state of being. In a world controlled by language, image, appearance, change and relativity, immediate power over people and events is the only possible result of deliberation and choice.

The plight of ethics in a sophisticated age thus turns on a central animating paradox: the power of pretense may indeed help us take advantage of the myriad minor hypocrisies and infidelities of mundane life; but it also guarantees that in the search for self we are always becoming someone else. Character is defined by circumstance. Situational ethics is no ethic at all. It is a rationalization, instead, for the primacy of means over ends, of relativity over permanence. The complex epistemologies of Plato, Aristotle, and a hundred other thinkers who attempt to fix the dialectic between individual being and social character are swept away in a sophisticated age by the pervasive present-mindedness of personality. Life on the ground is rarely controlled by rational systems of thought. The best solution we can make, law and jurisprudence, asserts the authority of mutable opinion over immutable ideals.

Power assumes a form characteristic of its use. It is established in the institutions of government, the system of governance and the body of laws. It is expressed in the relationships between people. It is embodied in the visage and manner of an individual. It conforms ultimately to the ancient definition of beauty. For power is the coordinate of form and function, the product of purposeful invention. It exists at the intersection of individual being and social character, where intentions meet circumstances.

Power is the root of ethics in our time. It is the dynamic energy that governs the relationship between men, as they are, as they can be, and as they hope to be. Success in our age is identified with power. It inheres in the effective attainment of ends, not in the righteous pursuit of means. The good life is defined purely by the productive quality of its actions. Ethical systems are judged according to principles of beauty rather than standards of rightness, by the affinity of conclusions for premises. They bear no relation to our age except as grounds for inventing a past that seems to explain present quandaries and solutions. The search for self must seek grounds for self-realization elsewhere. We have moved into an era that for good or ill ties all judgment to appearances.

CHAPTER SIX

Finding the Beautiful: The Primacy of Aesthetics in a Sophisticated Age

The epithet beautiful *is used by surgeons to describe operations
which their patients describe as ghastly, by physicists to
describe methods of measurement which leave sentimentalists
cold, by lawyers to describe cases which ruin all parties to them,
and by lovers to describe the objects of their infatuation,
however they may appear to the unaffected spectator.*

—George Bernard Shaw

*Intelligence demands beauty, but it must be an
intelligence that has the courage to see things through.*

—Leo Stein

THE SEARCH FOR SELF in a sophisticated age encounters many
difficulties, some peculiar to the ironic nature of dialectical inquiry and others peculiar to the paradoxical nature
of rhetorical self-consciousness. After all, it is one thing to argue
that self-knowledge comes from the active engagement of the
social context and quite another to know the difference between
self-knowledge and self-deception. How does one discover a
distinct identity amid the conflicting impressions of the crowd?
What safeguards prevent awareness of the self from being hi-
jacked by one aspect or another of our own complex social
character?

Our attempt to answer these questions benefits from the efforts of Socrates, who embarked on a similar quest amid the novelties and confusions of his own sophisticated culture. The Socratic search for self, as distinct from the Platonizing systems of thought that are premised on one aspect or another of Socrates' inquiry, is conducted in sympathetic understanding of the defects as well as abilities of human beings. Egotism, jealousy, anger and fear are a part of everyday life, Socrates would point out, but we need not succumb to them. They represent a special kind of mindlessness, the legacy of our animal origins. The destructive emotions are in no way unique attributes of individuality that can be ascribed to a higher order of being. When we act impulsively we behave according to the baser aspects of our nature. It is only when these inherited tendencies are subjected to the scrutiny of individual experience, to the power of thoughtful reflection, and to the heat of critical analysis that a person begins to express himself as a unique creature.

Integrated individuality is grounded in the complexities of *eros*, a special kind of love that originates in desire but transcends the carnality of the physical world. *Eros* propels the individual toward unity, first within himself and then with others. It is a quality of the soul quite unlike the destructive emotions which are enmeshed in physical actions and material effects. *Wholeness of being* is the goal of the Socratic search for self and, with characteristic irony, Socrates finds that the wholly self-conscious mind cannot exist in isolation from others. It is at once the product and producer of the *eros* that defines at any moment a discrete individuality within the tapestry of the crowd. This is a psychology of the most profound, contemporary type. It views the individual as a collection of many different selves each of which can be manifested through the emotions. We are different people in anger and in fear. We are truly ourselves only in love, but love broadly defined by *eros*. For self-knowledge is also a kind of self-love, and it must precede and activate our dealings with others if we are to have any hope of maintaining integrity in an ever-changing world of images and appearances. The love we commonly discover with someone else is but a contingent verisimilitude, a mutually accepted, agreeable illusion controlled everywhere by emotion and pretense. Intellect is alien to the lover and suspect to the beloved. It injects into courtship the tiniest bit of skepticism that, like rust on shining metal, eventually besmirches the superficial luster and eats away at the core. The problem of establishing individual being in the context of social character, of finding true *eros* amid the counterfeit emotions, ultimately comes to roost within the precincts of the activated mind.

145

The Primacy
of Aesthetics
in a
Sophisticated
Age

The Socratic irony—that self-knowledge is the product of social engagement—is compounded in our own age by the sophistication of self-consciousness. The search for self is everywhere confused and misdirected by powerful images, modern versions of the shadows that dance across the walls of Plato's cave. Relativity, opportunity and probability—the keys to personal power in an evolutionary sophistic regime dedicated to novelty—undermine the permanence and stability aspired to by every mind. The sophistic epistemology dictates that knowledge is of things and techniques, not of essences. It treats glimmering surfaces and topographical features rather than dense interiors. Contingent verisimilitude, the primary mode of perception and reality, obscures the pitted and roughened texture of daily life. Since they are self-contained units of reality, the verisimilitudes supplant substantial being as the center of understanding, appreciation and judgment. In a world where reality is based on transitory images, where history is an invention and consciousness is dominated by pervasive present-mindedness, *form* becomes the defining unit of being.

This principle inspires the contrived histories of contemporary life, personal as well as public. These can be appreciated for their symmetry, coherence and mindful artifice if not for their accuracy and factuality. History becomes poetry, an artful depiction of past events made to stand as metaphors for emotions and attitudes and beliefs of present importance. The tyranny of form also conditions how we judge the artificial constructions of politics. The ideal politician is the poet/statesman, the architect of structures and systems of political order. The poem of the sophisticated state is law. And the aim of law is order. We pay particular attention to the origins and derivations of law. This

makes it possible to govern ourselves within a formally constituted framework that balances power, rights and responsibilities. For the whole of public life is guided by the notion of
justice. And like Plato's republic, our own revolves around a
theory of harmonious interaction—the right alignment of all the
parts within the totality—between individuals and communities. In a similar spirit, education aims to produce a well-rounded
human being aptly fitted to the needs of production and citizenship. It seeks to enhance, that is, the potentialities of individual
being within the demands of social character. Finally, the potent
presence of form defines the contemporary conception of ethics
as an integrated structure of warrants and restrictions, rules and
guidelines. It is social harmony incarnate.

We respond in every case to the pleasing orderliness of the
well-wrought form. It is a phenomenon first noted by Aristotle
who, in the narrower compass of the *Poetics*, established an operational definition for artistic success. The excellent play, he
argues, is the one that achieves its effect through the proper
ordering of its parts. From this principle flows every judgment
that links form and function. From it we derive the still valid
notion that the highest state of being in art and in life is that
which can be described as "fitting" or "appropriate" or "proper"
to some end. Propriety, however, takes on an added dimension
in a sophisticated age. At the base of Aristotle's poetic—which is
essentially an art of making—lies the notion that the fitting and
the appropriate are ultimately measured in terms of *effectiveness*.
The well-wrought tragedy moves its audience to pity and fear.
The well-wrought state brings order out of chaos for the common benefit of its citizens. The well-wrought life brings action
into accord with virtue to produce happiness.

History, politics, education and ethics are poetic constructions valued more for a pleasing orderliness that aims toward
some end than for their factual content. They are *aesthetic* creations, artificial forms of perception and expression that embody
the dialectic between the being of individual self-knowledge
and the becoming of social self-assertion. The projection of the
self into history, politics, education and ethics is also an integrating experience that moves from disorder to unity. Above all

aesthetics involves the awareness of orderliness and the special power to instill order in thought, action and expression.

Aesthetics has traditionally been focused on the analysis of art, where the appreciation of specific artistic works turns ultimately on the perception of order and integrity. Although it is anachronistic to employ the term with respect to Plato and Aristotle, nearly every aspect of aesthetics was deeply considered by them. In particular, they introduced the concepts of *imitation* and *beauty* into the discussion of art, albeit in characteristically different fashions. The principles of artistic creation that Plato and Aristotle explored find wider application in our time. For in the sophisticated age aesthetics grows to encompass every realm of creativity and production.

Plato's aesthetic discussions appear principally in the *Ion*, *Symposium*, and *Politeia*. The *Sophist* and *Phaedrus* also contain relevant material. His aesthetic is bound up in his philosophical views about painting, sculpture, architecture, music and poetry. Dialectic is everywhere important to the analysis since Plato distinguishes the various crafts, which included everything from carpentry to statecraft, according to whether they are *acquisitive* or *productive*. The former result in the accumulation of goods or services. The latter, however, are further divided into the production of actual objects or the production of images. Images imitate their originals but cannot fulfill their functions, and Plato divides them into two kinds: genuine likenesses with the same properties as the model and semblances, apparent likenesses, which merely *look* like the original. This dialectical narrowing produces an important distinction, one that finds expression throughout the Platonic corpus. The making of deceptive semblances—like the use of perspective in painting—produces a false imitation that not only falls short of the original, but becomes something unique in itself.

The distinction between false and true imitation is troubling for Plato since imitation of any sort *ipso facto* falls short of the original. If it were perfect it would not be an image but yet another instance of the same thing. Therefore, all imitation exists in a duality. It is both true and untrue and so possesses simultaneously the qualities of being and non-being. As with other terms used by Plato, imitation expands and contracts with the movement of the dialectic. In its narrow sense, it encompasses paintings, dramatic poems, tragedy and songs as forms of imitation, or images. In its larger sense, it encompasses all created things since these are imitations of the eternal archetypes, the Forms. The world is alive with imitation. Language is a veil, appearances rule the day, seeming to be looms larger than being itself, at least to the uninformed senses. Art is placed at a further remove from the reality of the Forms in Plato's ordering of being, and exists at the lowest level of cognition. Then, again, some art is imitative in the negative sense, as deceptive semblance. The artists exiled from the perfect state do not possess a genuine craft like mathematics. They possess merely the knack to make things seem to be something else. Art, in this sense, is a cosmetic facility. Rhetoric shares this diminution of imitation, in Plato's eyes. It is the knack of self-conscious dissembling.

Aristotle takes another view of art and imitation. The *Poetics* contains what can be called his view of aesthetics although the work is primarily concerned with the art of making tragic dramas. Aristotle suggests two motives for tragedy. First, imitation is natural in man, and the mind automatically recognizes the tragic drama as a kind of imitation. Thus, in its most abstract form, as imitative art work, tragedy is pleasant because it leads one to learn through recognition, through identifying that such and such participate in the cognitive world. Second, tragedy is also an imitation of a special sort of object, fearful and pitiable events. The pleasure we feel when we watch the tragic play is from participating in this pity and fear by means of imitation. The pleasure of seeing the imitation overcomes the discomfort of observing the events themselves. This is perhaps the earliest definition of what we know as *aesthetic distance*. The audience knows the play to be an artificial creation and its pleasure comes from seeing how the artifice inspires deep-seated feelings within us.

Rather than finding that tragedy (and by implication all imitative art works) corrupts the mind, as Plato does, Aristotle argues that it helps men to be rational. For the vicarious participation of the audience leads to the purgation of emotions, a *catharsis*, that derives not from the immediate pleasure of observing skillful imitation but from tragedy's deeper psychological impact.

Both views of imitation—that it is a corruption of an ideal form and that it is a natural capacity of the human mind—spawn differing yet related conceptions of beauty. For Plato, the arts embody beauty in various degrees. Beauty is a perceived quality and so is open to change, deterioration and disappearance. It may appear to some but not to others. Behind the temporal embodiments of beauty, however, exists an eternal, absolute Form of beauty. Like the other Forms, that of beauty can be demonstrated by dialectic. And as with the other Forms, it can only be known partially through the senses. Still, it is more accessible than Forms such as justice or the good since the eye can discern aspects of the beautiful throughout the range of perception. Characteristically for Plato, the nature of the beautiful shifts according to the particular inquiry of specific dialogues. In some, the beautiful is identified with what is beneficial or what pleases through the senses. In others, the beautiful is identified with proportionate construction, of harmony between the parts, whether of a play, a state or a life.

Aristotle builds on Plato's notion of the beautiful, finding analogies for it in nature. The tragic play that can be described as beautiful, as artistically excellent, depends on the unity of its parts. It is organic, like the creatures of nature. It is the expression of its own internalized integrity, or wholeness. And it attains a sort of universality. Both the characters and the plot are plausible *and* probable. For Aristotle, the artistically superior play possesses verisimilitude in thought, speech and action.

But where Plato denies knowledge to the arts, Aristotle links it to the pleasurable effects of imitation. All men delight in knowledge, he avers, and it is the *delight* that distinguishes his conception of art from Plato's. Aesthetic ideas and effects in Plato are tied to some external standard of judgment, whether it is political, moral, or dialectical. Art does not exist as a separate thing in his ideal state, but is only to be valued for its utility in moral instruction. For Aristotle, however, aesthetic principles tie art to some internal aspect of specific types of art works—

epic poems, tragedy, lyric, music and the like. The products of poetic creation are to be judged like the products of nature, according to their unique structures, purposes and ends.

Mixtures of Platonic and Aristotelian ideas about art, imitation and beauty inhabit more formal treatments of aesthetic until Alexander Baumgarten's innovations in the 18th century. Baumgarten was the first to use the term *aesthetics* to designate that facet of mindfulness which involves knowledge gained through the senses, that is, the comprehension of the beautiful or the sublime, and Baumgarten sought to create a body of aesthetic knowledge comparable to the other disciplines of art and science. He thought aesthetics could in its own right be based on a set of first principles from which rules of performance and judgment could be derived. Aesthetic judgment could thus be predictive as well as descriptive.

The history of aesthetics since Baumgarten, however, has been marked by rejection of his notion that aesthetics is a principled discipline with characteristic rules and specialized subject matter. Moreover, it has also abandoned the search for beauty, at least as Plato, Aristotle and their successors conceived of it, to engage broader conceptions of the nature and purpose of art. To be sure, aesthetics is still regarded as the private preserve of intellectuals, critics and others of refined taste who seem to have acquired their aesthetic sensibilities through rigorous and rather effete training. The term has acquired a variety of technical meanings related to the interpretation of art works and to the explanation of beauty and sublimity. It is clothed in supposedly technical terms with seemingly precise definitions. It assumes the appearance of an established discipline. And behind it all— the studied remoteness, the refined opinions, the complex vocabularies—aesthetics seems to be based on rock solid notions about art, artists and the world. People have always argued about what constitutes "good" and "bad" art. Yet the modern aesthete rarely aims at Baumgarten's goal, the discovery of an essentially distinct science of aesthetics. Instead, he borrows ideas and concepts and words and ends from the other disciplines of human creativity in order not only to make statements about art but to make sense of it as well. Whatever their biases or preconceptions, seekers after the beautiful ground their claims in some systematic consideration of art as an activity, a product, an idea or an attitude.

With a twist of the critical kaleidoscope, aesthetics becomes now historical, now political, sociological, psychological, or ideological, according to the predispositions of the mind employing the terms and ordering the ends of aesthetic judgment. More significant, the commerce in aesthetics also travels in the other direction. Aesthetic ideas not only become integral parts of other disciplines such as history, politics, sociology, or psychology but these in turn become aesthetic systems of one sort or another, especially in the degree to which they attempt to explain order, coherence and integrity. It is this reflexive quality that accounts for the primacy of aesthetics in our time. Modern critics of art or life or politics often suppress the fact that they operate with aesthetics in mind. After all, no one but the scholar of art arrives at aesthetics in full awareness of its historic roots or even of the term itself. Baumgarten remains unknown and remote to critics who focus on products of human invention other than art. But the modern mind that seeks to put things in their place and to render them explicable arrives at aesthetics unknowingly and by default. Baumgarten's idea of the self-centered appreciation of art works can be generalized to cover all the products of human invention. Aesthetics grows to encompass the power of individual being to construct the contingent verisimilitudes that determine the interaction with others. In an age that has abandoned certainty, the aesthetic disposition offers the only hope for coherence.

That perhaps is the greatest outcome of the retreat from principles and rules. Aesthetics imposes a self-determined distance from the consequences of expression or action. It endorses a perceptiveness that pierces the fog of verisimilitude without importing extraneous moral considerations into the processes of appreciation and judgment. In a culture dominated by the sophistic principles of relativity, opportunity and probability, aesthetics is aptly suited to the needs of judgment without commitment to some overarching standard. Most important, it elevates the individual mind to the highest position in the hierarchy of thought and action. Personal judgment replaces social or communal or tribal codes as the basis of interaction. Effectiveness becomes the only sound measure of success in life and labor and learning.

The preoccupation with results accounts for our pride in the pragmatism of technology. Pragmatism itself is essentially an aesthetic view of life. Its introduction a century ago in the guise of a philosophical movement loosened the grip of metaphysics on moral, political and ethical speculation. It turned philosophy back to the problems of life as cognitive experience. It is no accident that the greatest proponent of pragmatism, William James, was an experimental psychologist before he became a pragmatic philosopher. Cognition and perception preoccupied his inquisitive mind long before he took up the questions of philosophy. Indeed, it was his discovery that the mind exists as both product and producer of the stream of consciousness that set up the basic intellectual premises of our present sophistication. Most important, pragmatism moved the discussion of ethics—the pursuit of the good life—from what *should be* to what *is*. The advent of pragmatism changed the calculus of judgment and appreciation in all the realms of human endeavor.

The intellectual innovations of the early 20th century transformed how individuals relate to communities and altered the relationship between being and becoming as fundamental ideas in philosophy. They mandated the emergence of aesthetics as the primary mode of criticism, comprehension and change. The appeal to higher principles has been replaced by the appeal to the interests and inclinations of the self, whether these are based in ignorance or intelligence. In all its incarnations—as history, psychology, or politics—aesthetics concerns the essentially private relationship between the perceiver and his judgments. It has become entirely personal. The failure to derive common principles makes it impossible to specify the consequences of aesthetic considerations except within the narrower boundaries of the borrowed language and concepts by which we express aesthetic judgments. In order to bring unity out of chaos, or at least to make it possible for critics of different attitudes, beliefs and vocabularies to talk to each other, we have invented *pluralism.* It is a concept that resonates with special meaning in the democratic climate of our sophistication. As a political principle, pluralism promotes equity and equilibrium if not justice. As a concept of literary criticism, it intends to heal the breach between critical systems. Pluralism serves as the aesthetic of aesthetics. As a concept of social criticism, pluralism introduces aesthetic relativity and the impossibility of final judgments into the debate on individual rights and communal responsibilities.

Art is valued less for its intrinsic qualities than for its impact and profitability, for its enjoyment and entertainment rather than its ideas. Moreover, art is now perceived as a transient phenomenon rather than an enduring product. It aims at the immediate gratification of the audience and the immediate financial satisfaction of the artist rather than for the benefit of future generations. It makes no pretense of durability or persistence or timeless universality, the qualities of art agreed upon by theorists of differing persuasions since at least Aristotle. Art is propelled by the same forces that control invention in every other realm of public life. Relativity, opportunity and probability are the central intellectual impulses controlling creativity and production. As a vestige of civilization and the human intellect, art no longer stands apart from the other products of human inventiveness. It is but one material expression vying for our attention and, more important, our financial support.

This transformation of art, from special expression to common utterance, signals a similar transformation in the nature and scope of aesthetics, not as a discipline of scholarly study, for that remains mired in traditional conceptions of art, but as a mode of perception and judgment. Aesthetics has been expanded to cover *every self-satisfying element of the human experience*. Its narrower meaning, as a *kind of knowledge* about technique or material or performance or whatever, has yielded to the broader concept of it as *a way of knowing*. For the aesthetic preoccupation with orderliness betrays an epistemological function aptly suited to life in a sophisticated culture. If aesthetics were merely concerned with things to be known, it would be incapable of telling us anything about the utility of knowledge in a shifting universe of values. However, the power to order the constituents of reality transcends the power merely to catalogue the data of experience. Thus, the aesthetic reality is expressed in the creations of art, the structures of the physical world, the organizations of business and government, the relationship between individuals and the psychological constructions of the mind. Aesthetics is an accounting, *a coming to terms with*, that stands outside the things to be known. It is experience itself.

Aesthetics, then, is as important as science to understanding our world. Both offer partial views of the buzzing actuality that surrounds us. Neither science nor aesthetics can promise omniscience; that is reserved for God, who is thought to be both inventor and artisan of the universe. Where science deals with parts and proceeds by hypothesis and experimentation, aesthetics deals with wholes and moves from concretion and factness. It is concerned with the self-evident object as a cause in itself, while science looks to the relations between things and behind causes.

Both aesthetics and science treat abstractions, but essentially different abstractions. The ultimate scientific abstraction is the atom, or even the sub-atomic particle, which is expressed by some mathematical formula. The ultimate abstraction of aesthetics is the symbol, which stands for something that can be concretely expressed in symbolic form. Science has its symbols, too, but these are merely signs external to the thing symbolized. The aesthetic symbol, however, is neither name nor label nor sign. It is a sample, a synecdoche, drawn from the object that is symbolized. As a way of knowing, science reveals the structures and functions that permeate the realm of experienced things. Aesthetics acquaints us with the world as it is related to our distinct selves. The aesthetic experience is never more important than, or independent from, our power to create contingent verisimilitudes—to order, that is, the reality that we choose to engage.

The fundamental difference between science and aesthetics is vivified in the way each employs language. The aesthetic symbol, since it is a sample and not a name, can never be in all ways precise. The comfortable ambiguities of art reside in the fact that although the artist always means what he says he never fully says what he means. The scientist, on the other hand, is always trying to express in absolute clarity and completeness the relationship between at least two factors. He tries to bring them into meaningful order among themselves and thus is constrained to make statements that are as lucid as possible. That is why science invents its own symbolic systems grounded in mathematics. In aesthetics, common language is the handmaiden to productive confusion. In science, it is an obstacle to precision.

Conceived as systems of knowledge, aesthetics and science provide complementary visions of life, one dealing with the artificial world and the other with the natural. We need look no further than the curriculum of an American university to see this distinction reflected in the division of labor between the arts and sciences. As ways of knowing, however, science and aesthetics are in severe imbalance. For sophistic culture moves from principles which are antithetical to science and at home in aesthetics. The commonplaces of our time—information is power, images are real, words are tools, change is inevitable, truth is relative—guarantee that the aesthetic attitude plays the central role in relating the realm of ideas to action as well as to art. The aesthetic sensitivity is cultivated within each one of us from the first time we become sensible of the world to the last moment that we are sentient at all.

This fact is at once a source of confidence and despair. On one hand, we revel in the power of appearances. By controlling the modes of expression—physical and emotional, intellectual and artistic—each of us has within our grasp the ability to reinvent who we are in the world of communal action. We can recast our social character to suit a mood, a circumstance, an expectation, a desire, or a fear. Few people do so with alacrity. Most people assume a characteristic personality shaped over time by the influences of circumstances and significant others. Nevertheless, as the ancient sophists were fond of demonstrating, each person is capable of the ecstatic transport of the self, of becoming beside himself in order to take advantage of opportunities for representation that lead to some immediate end. This is psychology transformed into art, drama projected into the realms of mundane life. The dominance of the contingent verisimilitude as the arbiter and determinant of reality guarantees that aesthetic judgments alone define our transient incarnations. We learn at an early age to assume a character, to script a role, and to act in the play of life as if individual being was but an imaginative fabrication. The mind has been liberated from the constraints of traditional social expectation by these intellectual inventions. It roams the artificial world of sophisticated society like some great predatory beast.

On the other hand, the power to reinvent social character carries with it an awful predicament. When the mind exercises its capacity to pretend and to imitate, it alters the conditions within which it will be perceived by others. For the relationship between individual being and social character is intense, immediate and mutually affective. Pretense and imitation become the sole realities in a sophisticated world. No wonder that the search for self has become such an elaborate and profitable industry for the proponents of self-help and such an entrenched problem for the self-defined sophisticate. The power to invent an external character can lead to a vacant selfishness and loss of integrity. The more it is exercised as an instrument of the external world, the less we know about our selves, either as separate entities or as participants in some larger community. Individual being is sucked into and obliterated by the manifold projections of social character.

Aesthetics is at once a way of knowing, a mode of perceiving and a method of expressing what we *feel* about ourselves and our world. It resides at the core of individual being and is at home among the emotions. It strives to make these intelligible and useful to the conduct of life. As a way of knowing, aesthetics acquaints us with an external world that is connected with our selves in ways too numerous to investigate completely. The aesthetic sense is discriminating. It allows us to order and to use what we discover. As a mode of perceiving, aesthetics permits the conscious self to assimilate experience without succumbing to either perpetual disorder or to arrested development. The former is the product of undisciplined curiosity, the latter, of overwhelming fear. As a method of expressing what we know or feel, aesthetics guides our use of language and images as technical devices and as instruments of social cohesion, change and communication.

The aesthetic sensibility plays on the paradox that animated Socrates' search after the self and enlivened Plato's ironic treatment of intelligence. Left to his own devices, a person has no more desire to know himself than to be known by others. Indeed, self-knowledge is always rendered inadequately. It is rooted more in self-justification than in the awareness of whole being. We indulge in selective repressions and avoidances, as much out of necessity as out of willful manipulation.

The contingent verisimilitude lies at the heart of the aesthetic experience, for it exerts the power of individual being as protector as well as creator of realities. We do not so much avoid self-knowledge as condition it. The modern sophistries of self-improvement, self-empowerment and self-assertion focus our attention on the techniques of *playing the role* of the self-knowing being. Courage now resides in the ability to act out these truncated roles in the face of our ignorance about our self and our many selves. The aesthetic experience is constituted by the individual coming to terms with himself through the examination of art, politics, history and the like. The search for self that Socrates pursued was animated by a belief that there is a truth although it may never be clearly or completely perceived. Too many things get in the way—human fallibilities and foibles, imprecise words, animal emotions, overwhelming and narrow self-interest—for the journey to reach a wholly satisfying conclusion. A hunger remains even after the banquet of dialectical inquiry has been served.

The search for self is essentially the quest of the artist played out in the context of society. We tend to think of artists as eccentric and unreliable pursuers of some ineffable truth, who seek to render what they find in the inadequate but expressive materials of their art. *Interpretation*, in the form of criticism and assessment, has become so important precisely because art of any kind admits of ambiguities. Interpretation now overwhelms artistic expression as the primary mode of social commentary. We thrive on the analysis of *expression*, whether it is a Presidential speech, a movie, a book or the utterances of a lover. But the price of our accommodation to flux and fluidity has been the abandonment of the *products* of human creativity for a preoccupation with the *processes* of production. Criticism has supplanted art as the primary determinant of culture in our sophisticated age.

Since aesthetics is concerned with the comprehension of symbols that are in themselves parts of larger wholes, the self serves as an integrator, interpreter and communicator. Shaded one way, these terms find a home in contemporary psychology where integration, interpretation and communication are the major constituents of the healthy mind. Shaded another way, these terms find a home in contemporary sociology, where they are major components of the efficiently functioning community. In fact, whether it is concerned with the appreciation of art or the understanding of organization or the comprehension of the mind, the aesthetic experience is essentially rooted in the primary behaviors that the social sciences dissect, analyze and reconstitute in their own special terms. The aesthetic self subsumes all others since it is an instrument for elaborating experience.

Indeed, this view broadens not only aesthetics, to encompass ideas and actions and organizations as well as works of art, but also the concept of *artifact*. These are not only the products of the characteristic media of artistic expression, books, cinema, video and music; they are also the tools and devices that empower technology, the political structures of community that guide our social interaction, the commercial arrangements that determine prosperity and well-being, the systems and methods and curricula of the schools, and the codes of behavior that constitute ethics. The contingent verisimilitudes of individual being and social character, founded as they are on manufactured images and impressions, constitute the fundamental artifacts of our sophistication. We leave behind us impressions and images of ourselves, our values, our beliefs, our hopes and our fears as potent and disturbing as the wake of some great ship passing through calm seas. Life is a series of interrelated experiences that is made significant only by our inventions and interpretations. It has become truly artificial. It is the residue of numerous and incalculable interventions by ourselves and by others on the processes of degeneration that affect the body, the mind and the soul.

The aesthetic appreciation of life constitutes an acceptance of our very personal reaction to ambiguity and confusion. It aims to avoid despair, but not at all costs. Repression, avoidance and denial are explicable in the context of aesthetics but they do not support a self-determined view of things that brings intelligence to bear on the problems of life. Reality is a succession of dramatic enactments by individuals intending in every instance to fulfill immediate desires or ends.

The primacy of aesthetics is dictated by our valuing of pretense and imitation as the primary impulses of history, politics, education and ethics. To be sure, the shift to aesthetic standards of appreciation and judgment, which emphasize formal beauty and final effectiveness, has liberated the inventive capacity of the individual mind. It has freed us from outworn strictures of behavior and has aimed us in the direction of experimentation and risk. It has awakened us to the power of the mind to create an operational reality and has relieved us from worrying about the conundrums of metaphysics, theology and religion. The aesthetic sensibility has placed each of us at the center of things, far more than any humanistic philosophy of the past.

Not only has art succumbed to aesthetics (and works of art to works of criticism) but life as an organized pursuit has become a totally aesthetic experience as well. We are confused by this because we still attempt to explain ourselves in terms and concepts that draw their power from other, superseded rationalizations. The paradoxes of sophistic culture condemn us to a mean-spirited and cynical adaptation of ends to means in the never-ending accommodation of inevitable changes and relative truths. Our self-styled dramas lack the transcendental qualities of great tragedy, where the issues are clearly drawn and the flaws of the tragic figure so completely known. We also lack the permanent cultural illusions of less sophisticated societies from which it is possible to be alienated or banished. Alienation and banishment are folded into the operations of a culture based on appearances, change and relativity. The ancient myths no longer hold. They provide no aesthetic base for self-evaluation and self-correction. Like the Greeks, we have cast our lot with the vagaries, temptations, promises and hopes of man-made reality. In our weaker moments we might succumb to hubris and believe that we, too, can be gods. But the presumption is short-lived, the self-confidence ill-borne. Life is always hemmed in by the assertions of others and their expectations of us.

CHAPTER SEVEN

The Fruits of
Our Sophistication

*Innovations abound, are looked for, expected. Foreigners, distin-
guished and undistinguished, have flocked to the city to make money,
to make reputations, to pose. There is a sense of novelty, criticism,
and reorganization, rather than a sense of steadiness and assured
progress. There is intellectual acuteness without intellectual
certainty. There is a high degree of enlightenment and sophistication,
but little sense of security. And the upsetting of security seems to
have begun recently and to be still in progress . . . . Here was an
astonishing and at times reckless outburst of energy rushing to a
multiple perfection. It was a period of achievement following
achievement and not a period of consolidating gains—a restless and
a brilliant time which dwarfed precedent times and made them look
poor indeed . . . . In such a society there is often reckless eagerness for
entertainment, cultivation, and for being up-to-date. It has its
groups of intellectuals, its sophists, who invade the metropolis with
their propagandas and their ministry of improvement . . . . And to be
polite and urbane had reached . . . a high degree of sophistication.*

—F. J. E. Woodbridge

OUR SOPHISTICATION, LIKE THAT of the Greeks, cuts both ways.
On one hand, it makes possible material wealth and
individual enrichment by emphasizing novelty, criticism and reorganization. On the other hand, it undercuts the
very basis of community and fellowship by imperiling stability,
common values and traditional beliefs. The sophistication of
culture is a Faustian bargain of epic proportions that is being

played out in our time in history, politics, education, ethics and aesthetics. These are the realms of self-consciousness, self-expression and self-realization now defined by rhetoric.

Plato realized as much, of course, for the Athens described by Woodbridge forms the backdrop of his dialogues. Plato was an enemy of restless energy. He had observed too well what mischief derived from the rhetorical relativity of sophistic thought. And his use of Socrates as the dramatic foil of the sophists in his dialogues parallels his use of the Socratic method to examine and channel what he perceived to be the combustible emotions of his community. Plato was troubled by the human *becoming*, the sophisticated mind that turns outward to the social world before it understands the dimensions of its own reality. His dialogues encapsulate the conditions that produce neurosis in the individual and chaos in society, that prevent the full attainment of individual being and emphasize too greatly the power of social character. For him, the sophisticated mind's hyperactive immaturity—what we would call innovation or originality—leaves an indelible mark on the structures and institutions of social life and forever alters the destiny of individuals. The death of Socrates is the emblem for Plato of the sophisticated wrong-headedness and communal madness that led to the demise of Athens itself. The human *being* has been consumed by the rush for advantage, success, power and sophistication. The city governed by Socratic wisdom can only be realized in the utopia of the *Politeia*.

Plato's dialogues portray a subtle but powerful point about the sophists and their programs of improvement: sophistication is paradoxical. In its paradoxes lie the keys to its success as well as the seeds of its destruction. It treats of power over other people, of single-mindedness over culture and community. Yet it succeeds only in the degree to which each mind participates in its contingent verisimilitudes as if they were all that can ever be known. Sophistication is propelled by self-confidence, but it inspires a pervasive skepticism that fuels self-doubt. It is egocentric, but looks outward to a world populated by many self-interested beings who need allies in order to accomplish ends beyond their immediate powers. Sophistication is a process of disillusionment as well as enlightenment, of the abandonment of unknowable ideals for realizable, rationalized aims. It brings both knowledge and sorrow. It reduces communal behavior to rules and laws but values individuality above conformity. Sophistication deals with the surface of things. It ranks the apparent over the real, the exterior over the interior, as the basis for judging success in life, labor and learning. It perpetually conceives of the present as dynamic, mutable, overwhelming.

Sophistic paradox breeds crisis. It leads to the breakdown of traditional values and beliefs by vivifying the relative differences between individuals, nations and races. In turn, it causes the collapse of central authority in all realms of thought and action by replacing the traditional foundations of social order with the requirements of individual success. The breakdown of values and the collapse of central authority spur changes in the organization of communities, in how people conceive of collaboration and self-interest. New communities emerge that transcend geographical and political boundaries since they are defined only by the capacities for communication. Finally, the chaos of the present leads to a fascination with the past. It engenders the intellectual return to some Golden Age that exists only in the imagination of the mind pining after order. Sophistication thus pulls us in two directions at once, foward to an uncertain future composed of infinite possibilities and back to an all-too-certain past of nonexistent actualities.

Sophistic paradox is pervasive. Great hope for the future of human kind confronts within each of us the gnawing fear that our own personal destiny is somehow incomplete and inadequate. There is a growing sense among us that things are spinning out of control. The only absolute we have been able to invent is the pervasive relativity that now dominates science, art, education, politics, ethics and aesthetics. Although we enjoy a wealth of facts about a myriad of topics we also suffer a dearth of integrating wisdom to bind what we know into comprehensible wholes. The more we learn about things the less we seem to understand them, either in themselves or in their relations to each other. Our inventors and entrepreneurs increase the products of our confusion and multiply the effects of our unease. The infinite extension of human knowledge, our self-defined purpose for the intellectual life, bangs up against the finite constructions of human expression. Our many languages—technical, formal, colloquial, social, theological, mathematical, visual, scientific— fragment reality and condemn the simplest acts of communication to inarticulate incoherence. Profound uncertainty not only undermines individual self-confidence, it also weakens our efforts to establish standards of conduct that guide how human beings treat each other as individuals as well as members of communities. We seem to be so busy with innovation that we are incapable of meaningful introspection or useful integration. Novelty has become the hallmark of the times while familiarity breeds not only contempt but boredom.

Sophistic paradox is profound. The temporal, material and artificial—not the eternal, spiritual and natural—guide daily life. Success is measured exclusively by wealth, material excess or excessive zeal in the pursuit of immediate ends. The intangible aspects of leading the good life fall out of the organized pursuit of politics, education and ethics. The alarming, stimulating singularity of a highly developed individual consciousness gives way to the comfortable, unthreatening familiarity of the group and the soft appeal of a pleasing disposition. "Likability" emerges as the primary virtue of the public life each of us is forced to construct from the raw materials of our own character. A passionless pseudo-objectivity replaces the subjective emotional realities of living life among competing and only partially formed fellow beings always in a state of becoming. Life is conducted in the third person, as if each of us stands outside not only the hubbub of daily affairs, observing and choosing yet never engaging, but also outside of ourselves like actors waiting for the cue to perform. This feigned detachment is a learned response. It is inculcated early in the educational process and cultivated by a society that thrives on imitation, impersonation and improvisation. Coming to terms with sophistication ultimately entails coming to terms with the images upon which it is based. It demands suppressing the mind's natural inclination to pierce to the core of things and to deal instead with surfaces and superficialities as if they are all that is or can ever be. Manipulation, not understanding, is the goal of self-consciousness. It is better not to sense too keenly the contradictions among the competing images of reality that inundate the senses. Like some modern day Icarus, the mind that soars too near the sources of paradox can end up plummeting with melted wings into the wine dark sea.

The crisis of sophistication turns on the question of personal and communal *identity*. Plato's dialogues are constructed around the search by individuals for the universal constituents of their reality, for the commonplaces of mind that bind them together despite their unique characters. Plato's Athens is the creation of a mind searching for the *ethos* of a people who share a common history and location but who are uncertain about a common future. His great art, of course, resides in the fact that he knew how the search would end. Socrates exists in Plato's imagination as a literary figure, the actual man having been dead for decades. The city has passed from greatness. Plato fashions his response to the paradoxes of sophistication from the residue of Athens' recent disastrous history.

Identification has assumed central importance for us because our culture is always in the midst of inventing itself anew according to circumstances and needs that carry only present significance. Ours is a reality with shifting centers and an unclear focus. We seek our individuality in the ever-changing precincts of social character, where personal identity is tied to the externalities of job, profession, education, race, sex, marital status, wealth. The puzzlements of our sophisticated age penetrate even the most mundane affairs. When faced with a contradiction, we fall back on a principle of medieval logic. We make a distinction. The sophisticated world is constructed of such distinctions. These are the atomic elements of the contingent verisimilitudes that control our relations with each other. And the mind in all its manifestations—as leader or follower, producer or consumer, innovator or imitator, author or audience—constantly strives to exercise an ancient power over these external confusions. It seeks to bring order out of chaos.

Despite our cleverness, the solutions we invent to the paradoxes of an increasingly complex, rapidly changing, man-made universe ultimately confront the central paradox of our time:

however intricate or sophisticated they may be, our solutions are only temporary responses to a permanent situation. Einstein, not Newton, uncovered the foundations of our reality. Time is now measured by the orbit of an electron around its nucleus rather than by the revolution of the planets around the sun. The result has been a collapse of causes and effects, a compression of time to such a degree that all sense of antecedents and consequences is lost in the blur of a continually unfolding present. The thinking being who struggles to make sense of things can only observe what has happened, perhaps note it for future reference and then pass on to the next event. All speculation becomes historical in an age possessed by novelty. No wonder there is intellectual disenchantment amid economic and material plenitude. The tools of the mind, our own wings of wax, are ill forged for the task. They shift and change in order to accommodate, if not anticipate, the underlying turbulence that defines the present. For the mind that bothers to penetrate the veneer of everyday life, the problem is more essential and less clear than it first seems. It is rooted in a vague distress with the basis of reality itself and it draws us back to the question that has intrigued sensitive minds throughout the ages. What constitutes *being* in a world always on the verge of *becoming* something else?

It is an unpopular question to pursue these days amid the mercenary philosophies that dominate sophisticated culture. It smacks of metaphysical perplexity. No answer can be turned to profit. Consideration of it only leads to discomfort and perhaps disillusionment. Moreover, the metaphysician approaches the inquiry loaded with debt to the divinely inspired minds of the past. He ends up constructing a finely wrought system of explanations and excuses as ornate as it is inapplicable to life on the ground. We become pragmatists by default as well as by choice. Nothing else seems to work in a world where statement and action are interchangeable constitutents of a reality based in appearances and communicated in emotive language and images. The common tendency among pragmatic thinkers is to recast the distinction between being and becoming. "To be" becomes "to do" and the defining perspective turns on the requirements and consequences of profitable action. That at least poses a manageable dilemma, for it allows us to ask questions and define problems for which we already have solutions.

The struggle to establish order amid chaos is closely connected to the dilemma of *being* some *one*, of standing out in the crowd, of possessing a distinctive character and purpose. The conundrum of individuality discloses the archaic origins of paradox itself. For it engages at every turn the distinction between similarity and difference, the most rudimentary of concepts that organize philosophic speculation, political ideology and scientific investigation. Our initial unpopular question about the nature of personal being in a universe of change leads to others that thinkers since at least Plato have pursued in one form or another. How did we come to be as we are? What does our knowledge of the past tell us about the present and our prospects for the future? Who are we? In the continuing dialogue between the individual and his culture there emerges the most important query of all. Who am I?

The search for identity is covered over by the awesome inventiveness of our sophistication. It is conducted off to the side, almost by accident, but it pierces to the heart of being in every aspect of conscious life. For the seeker of individual identity, of what we call the self and the ancients called the soul, must also survey the larger regions of community and communication within which self-consciousness is bred and exercised everyday. To reveal one's self ultimately entails discovering the fundamental connections that bind individual being to social character.

In an age of sophistication, rhetoric assumes the central responsibility for the statement of reality, the organization of society and the instigation of change. It emerges as the primary instrument in the search for identity. For the commonplaces of rhetorical self-consciousness support the rise of sophistication as a habit of mind, a mode of perception and a form of behavior. And though our sophistication is premised on a very few notions, these animate the questions, underwrite the methods, organize the systems and dictate the solutions to the problems of history, politics, education, ethics and aesthetics. We behave according to these commonplaces although we may state them differently, oppose them vigorously and deny them honestly. Advocates of sophistication and simplicity alike are forced into intellectual channels controlled by the precepts of a rhetorical world. Words are tools. Images are real. Information is power. Change is inevitable. Truth is relative.

On one hand, we use rhetoric to critique established ways of thinking and to reformulate the problems of life in community. Motivated by the belief that an essential component of thought and action has yet to be realized, we produce new ways of moving from analysis to articulation and action. These new systems, methods and paradigms are essentially rhetorical inventions. They become real when others are convinced of their validity or potency. They pass away when we lose confidence in their power and promise. That is a far different notion of reality than the one we sometimes wish would prevail, that behind the confusion of human utterance exists an unchangeable, firm, eternal order of being. But in a sophisticated culture, reality is that which can be agreed upon, acted upon and counted on. Sophistication is mindful, not mindless, in its operations. In a world where anything is probable, everything is possible.

On the other hand, our sophistication is an exercise in nostalgia on an international scale. Based in figurative language and the stylistics of rhetorical presentation, it resurrects the symbols of a mythic past and invests them with contemporary significance. We rarely address fundamental questions of religion, morality, community or individual being. Instead, the modern sophist grows immensely rich reconfirming the prejudices of his audiences, whatever the topic or setting. He may promise to empower his auditors but he points out that power resides not in the freedom of the mind but in the enslavement of the tongue. Verbal and imagistic display, with the aim of pleasing rather than challenging the audience, is the primary motive for their work. Stability is absolutely basic to our sophistication, for it confronts the challenge of perpetual change in every sphere. Our sophists not only defend the existing political and social orders. They participate in them and profit from them.

Paradoxically, our sophistication has led to a weakening of confidence in the pattern and meaning of life, despite the fact that we exercise our ordering inventiveness every day. It seems to be easier for one mind to lose track of itself, to become lost among the clutter of expressions and actions that constitute the real world, the rhetorical world, of sophisticated society. We have invented numerous healing disciplines that attempt to provide the individual mind with a sense of self equal to the artificial instruments that implement individual will. These are but contingent verisimilitudes, however, complicated ways of "seeming to be" that are fitted with intricate methods of analysis and extensive descriptive vocabularies. They each substitute one kind of order for the apparent disorder of modern life. And they can veer sharply toward the mysticism of religion on one hand or the positivism of psychology on the other. Life in an age of sophistication demands mechanisms and attitudes that integrate individual initiative into a scheme of social order. Despite differences in method, manner and end they derive in one way or another from rhetoric. For the modern arts of psychological or sociological analysis all turn on the discrepancies between what we say, what we mean and what we do.

Consequently, as a verbal art of persuasion and as a structuring art of action, rhetoric now serves three functions. Each is a cognate to some specific social science but is never totally contained within any one of them. Instead, the fundamental functions of rhetorical sophistication determine the specific reification of rhetoric that emerges in the context of particular historic circumstances and needs. They are all present and active, singly or together in one form or another. They contribute to the breakdown of traditional moral values. They guide the critique and reformation of authority in all realms of human activity. They result in the restructuring of traditional social and political orders. And they foster a new international culture based in sophisticated self-confidence and expressed in sophisticated forms of self-expression. The functions of rhetoric are at once ancient and modern, novel and known. For like all things rhetorical, they embody the paradoxes of our sophistication. Each is a realm of "seeming to be."

First, rhetoric exercises a *propaedeutic* function. As a verbal art of persuasion, it seeks to discover commonalities in order to prepare the ground for communication. Arguments are elaborated to elicit assent at every stage. One set of conclusions becomes the premise for the next line of reasoning. As an art for structuring and exercising power, rhetoric analyzes the potential for change and invents the mechanisms for common action. Processes, methods, systems, organizations and institutions are constructed to resolve dissent and implement common agreement. The two incarnations of rhetoric, as verbal art and structuring art, are folded into each other. For the structures of power require argumentation and persuasion. Varied as it may be in terms of content and objective, sophistication is a process that seeks to prepare individual minds for communal action. Rhetoric inspires a new kind of politics by reforming and broadening an ancient institution, the *polis*. It also gives birth to a new form of education by reconstituting the ancient curriculum, the *paedia*.

Second, rhetoric serves a *hermeneutic* function. Disagreements about "what was," "what is," and "what can be" involve competing claims about what constitutes the facts of reality. The rhetorical mind not only sifts and analyzes what it apprehends. It also orders what it discovers into bodies of useful knowledge that compose at any one moment what can be called the sophistic epistemology. Our sophistication is powered by signs, symbols and images as well as by words. Ambiguity and confusion are the norm. Out of necessity each of us practices a kind of hermeneutics every day as we navigate between the often discordant languages of technology, art and politics. The significance of modern life often lies buried beneath the images we invent to communicate specific feelings or ideas or desires or, conversely, we devise to hide our real intentions. Language is inadequate to thought and emotion but we have no choice in the matter. Knowing that the world is fated to perpetual, universal uncertainty, the sophisticated mind revels in the duplicities and infidelities of modern semantics. Things are never as they seem to be, things are only as they seem to be. Interpretation is a fundamental skill for survival amid sophistication.

Finally, rhetoric has a *therapeutic* role, not only as an art of composition and expression but also as an instrument of social change and artistic renaissance. Revolutions in science and in politics are framed in new terms and new concepts that reflect a shift in the meaning of traditional relationships between ideas, words and action. Rhetoric brings language into accord with the new realities. It expresses facts and is a cause for their invention as well. Rhetoric is both an attitude about the world and a structure for language and performance that produces a new awareness of the power of the creative mind.

Preparation, interpretation and correction are key activities in the pursuit of self-knowledge and self-confidence. They recast the social world according to individual intentions. They are the basis for change in the way people regard their circumstances and their futures. And they are internalized intellectual processes that provide each mind with an assessment of its position among others. The search for self is always vibrating between the temptations of "seeming to be" and the rigorous demands of "being." Novel and technological as it may seem, our sophistication is rooted in the educational programs of ancient Greece and Rome, where utility and relativity determined the value of the individual. Gorgias and Protagoras did much to liberate the human spirit from the confines of superstition and blind acceptance of the mythic tradition. They showed us that the world could indeed be made in our image, that the creative power of the mind unleashed was the most potent component of the cosmos. Yet their inventions and arguments set loose contradictory impulses that to this day order the way we think about life and its possibilities.

Plato, Aristotle and the sophists sought to ground the necessary conditions of *being human* in the inventive powers of the mind. The reduction to self-consciousness led each to a conception of social order and progress rooted in the persuasive dynamics of language. The complex solutions they each devised have often been portrayed as dialectical oppositions—Plato's idealism set against sophistic pragmatism, Aristotle's verbal reality against Plato's Theory of the Forms, sophistic self-confidence against Socratic self-doubt. But they actually represent the continuum of all possible relationships between thought, expression and action. That spectrum, in turn, has illuminated the manifold variations of Western thought ever since. In the

150 years between the birth of Socrates and the death of Aristotle, Western civilization acquired the paradoxes and contradictions that are the hallmark of life in a sophisticated age. The rise of sophistication, whatever its proximate cause, is always accompanied by the unique flowering of individual initiative amid social crisis and the assertion of individuality as the primary component of social order.

Sophistication is founded on individual choice. The *human becoming* is always in a state of transition, for good or ill. Choosing is the primary activity of consciousness. It is impossible not to choose. Even passivity in the face of multiple choices is a form of choosing. Sophisticated societies are marketplaces dedicated to the distribution of goods and services, ideas, ideologies, lifestyles, philosophies, methods and systems. Sophistication, after all, is a *process* as well as a *state of mind*. Consequently, sophistication tends toward chaos, since only the intentions of the inventing mind bring momentary order to the flow of consciousness. The pace and raw necessities of modern life undercut the introspective tendencies of the mind seeking itself. Thoughtful analysis, tempered speech, reasonable expectations, and the contemplative life in general find no place in the pandemonium of a world powered by human cleverness and the demand for immediate gratification. Indeed, introspection and self-awareness are rarely valued in the sophisticated world. Idealism is regarded as naive and naivete is mistaken for idealism.

We apparently confront three choices in the creation of self. Each is an expression of dissociation. Isolated and radicalized, each leads to peculiar forms of anti-social behavior. Throughout the day, however, most people constantly choose one or another of these alternatives—singly or together, consciously or not, at one time or another—in order to maintain at least the semblance of individual integrity in a world governed by change, relativism and the contingent verisimilitudes of rhetorical self-consciousness.

First, you can *abdicate* your position in community, a radical dissociation that turns away from the manifold contingent verisimilitudes of sophistic culture and toward self-absorption. This is the choice of monks and madmen, who represent two extreme accommodations by abdication. But abdication can occur selectively and in smaller doses. We withdraw from social contact on a variety of levels and for a variety of reasons. Abdication is certainly the choice of that half of the population who do not vote in general elections and, by so doing, abandon their share of personal and communal sovereignty. It is also the choice of those who participate in the new monasticism of cults and private religions, of the sophisticated self-help movements like EST, the Forum, Scientology and the like. The monastic life need not represent deprivation and poverty. More likely than not, it is peddled on the promise of financial well-being, the secret knowledge of success, the triumph over alienation and despair. In abdication, personal being is asserted paradoxically, by denying the validity of one sophistic verisimilitude while participating in another. In the extreme, abdication takes the form of self-destruction, the self-induced obliteration of self by whatever means.

Second, you can *subordinate* yourself to the pervasive contingent verisimilitudes set loose on the world by other people. This is the corporate ideal, the choice of the good citizen, and what can be called the "worker bee syndrome." Someone, after all, must keep the hive cool, the nectar flowing and the Queen bee serviced. Subordination entails few risks and has its own ample material rewards. It is a process of giving up by degrees, of accepting one condition in order to foster another—working at an odious job, for example, in order to raise a family or pursue an avocation or hobby. The subordinate person loses all sense of self as an independent, inventive being. He merely exists in a constant state of becoming, tied to some external determinant of reality, struggling to perform according to impossible standards and values. In subordination, personal being flows from the passive participation in the sophistic realities, life's contingent verisimilitudes. In the extreme, subordination takes the form of radical self-effacement, the obfuscation of individuality.

Finally, you can *dominate* other people by creating your own contingent verisimilitudes. This is the choice of the sophists who, as we have seen, believe that it is not only in your power but also in your interest to create your own realities. Domination motivates all kinds of sophistries, those that claim to be sophisticated as well as those that are apparently unsophisticated. For it is another paradox of sophistication that since it is primarily a verbal phenomenon, where the mastery of language determines the shape of reality, it can simultaneously support and attack contrary incarnations of itself. Religious fundamentalism, political and philosophical absolutism, and professional or social or intellectual elitisms of all kinds (even those advertised as egalitarian) construct contingent verisimilitudes that either stand outside of or subsume or contradict the tenets of sophistication. All the while they use the tools and techniques of rhetoric to assert their unique righteousness. In domination, individual being grows out of the personal realization of the sophistic verisimilitudes, whatever they may be. In the extreme, domination takes the form of militant self-assertion, or hubris, the elevation of self over everything else.

Each of these accommodations seems to be an exercise of individual choice. The abdicator is articulate about the causes for his disengagement from society. It is all connected, he tells us, to the demands of some overarching ideology or philosophy or political policy. Abdication is self-improvement, he claims, since it allows him to exercise his integrity and saves him from enslavement to some other contingent verisimilitude. The subordinator has reasons aplenty—family, career, obligations to society—to stay lashed to the wheel. His integrity grows in the service to others, he argues. Subordination performed willingly and openly is a virtue. The dominator brags about his clever use of power, his manipulation of the system for his own ends, his hegemony over others. Domination is the sign of success among the sophisticated. Besides, he argues with a wink and a nod, he can give it up whenever he wants, it's really not that important. Others may be addicted to power; his use is proscribed by some noble end. Yet each explanation is an excuse and not a reason, a pathetic defense of the pattern of personal choices in face of an inevitable, irresistible fate.

Abdication, subordination and domination are accommodations to the paradoxes of sophistication. They are compromises in the search for self that embody different aspects of dissociation. Abdication separates us from the society or community or group that can define, nurture and promote us. Subordination separates us from our own impulses and feelings, thoughts and spirit. Domination separates us from other people by making them objects to be manipulated rather than recognizing them as fellow sentient beings. In each case we devise the semblance of being to mask the fact that we are in reality always in a state of becoming. None of these accommodations, however, can support an ethical system that maintains its principles despite changes in the world of action. Ethics is dead. Our substitute for it, a finely crafted and cumbersome legal system, is as close as we can get to providing a standard of conduct for all people. Since they admit the ambiguities of our times into the very notions upon which they are founded, the legalisms of our age are always open to dispute. Such is the genius and the madness of sophistication. Even its fundamental principles are controlled by the commonplaces of inevitable change, pervasive relativity, the domination of appearances and the power of emotional symbols, words and images.

But the search for self amid the turmoil of sophistication, innovation and ambition usually begins at the wrong end. It presumes the existence of a self that is somehow reflected in, or obscured by, the manifestations of social character. And it sees the task as one of disentanglement and refinement, of isolating the essential characteristics of the individual from the noise of his associations.

Informed choices, however, come from self-examination conducted in the hurly-burly of daily life. There is an alternative to abdication, subordination and domination that can guide the mind looking after itself. This alternative path to self-knowledge involves what can best be called a navigational sense since it produces no final answers. It merely yields a clearer understanding of the way to proceed in the search after individual being at any single point in the development of the mind. This fourth accommodation to sophistication has been entangled in the long course of Western history with both religion and science, faith and skepticism. It has engendered autocracies and democracies. It has supported the individual against the state and, at other times, the state against the individual. When it is successfully pursued, this fourth path leads neither to systematic philosophy nor to intellectual anarchy. It is the most arduous accommodation to sophistication, yet it resides in the simplest of human behaviors. It goes by many names in our time since it seems to be the basis of "New Age" thinking in psychology, philosophy and politics. But it is deeply rooted in the paradox that has come to be called the choice of Socrates.

Socrates has been celebrated for his self-doubt and his self-confidence. He has been called the father of idealistic philosophy and identified as idealism's first skeptic. He has been accused of divorcing philosophy from real life and praised for being the first and truest practical philosopher. Even in his lifetime he was regarded as both a sophist and the sophists' strictest opponent. We know him best through Plato, our main source of information about the man and his methods. Plato began his own investigations into reality and knowledge hewing close to the grain of Socrates' thought. But over time Plato began to enunciate a complex and ornate theory of knowledge, a cosmology really, that transcends Socrates' own admittedly meager efforts. Thus, Plato's dialogues at once portray and transform the character of Socrates for other purposes. And even though Plato's dramatic character Socrates never comes to firm conclusions about the things he investigated, the historic Socrates clearly believed that rigorous dialectical examination leads to an honest-to-god plain truth.

Things are never what they seem to be, Socrates argued, and he made it his profession to examine anyone who claimed to possess wisdom of any sort, rich citizens, generals and prominent sophists such as Hippias, Gorgias and Protagoras. He questioned their statements and assumptions about knowledge, courage, truth, beauty, morality and piety. The result was usually confusion about the very nature of the virtues that were assumed to be the foundations of civic cooperation and personal excellence in Athens. It was a productive confusion, according to Socrates, since it illuminated the substantial ignorance that rules our lives and provided the starting point for the apprehension of true wisdom and self-understanding. He earned many adherents and perhaps many more enemies. Socratic doubt, embodied as it was in a kind of prosecutorial inquisitiveness, too closely resembled the sophistic logic-chopping that shook Athenian society during the fifth century B.C.

Socratic doubt is also premised on a paradox and is therefore not only difficult to understand but also to use as a practical guide in the search for self. I am only wise, Socrates claimed, because I know that I am ignorant. In Plato's hands the paradox becomes the irony that animates the early dialogues, where Socrates confronts sophistic confidence in unresolved arguments about the nature of virtue. Behind Plato's creation, however, stands a man with a singular purpose. Socrates lived his response to sophistic relativism, inevitable change and the contingent verisimilitudes of rhetoric. He searched long and hard for beliefs that were unshakable, turning over first this one then that one, examining them all with the intensity of a child looking for crabs under rocks at the beach. He, too, was constantly running between skepticism and sophistry, appearance and reality, because for him leading the good life depended on a never-ending search for the truly vital among the merely vicarious. Whatever he is called, philosopher or sophist, Socrates was first and foremost a thinking being whose reflections on the paradoxes of life have come to us in the guise of many philosophies.

By recognizing that every question has at least two sides, Socrates started Western thought on its merry chase after certitude, finality and unification. He did not stop with that discovery, however. After all, even the sophists knew as much. Rather, he pushed through to the farther side of relativism, to see that both common opinions and proven doctrines become static, stale and moribund when they are left unexamined. Our examination of them reveals the real similarities among the apparent differences that distinguish the truth, however stated, from mere opinion. Our search for self is always mediating between uncertainty about the higher purpose of human kind— the shoulds and oughts of moral law—and confidence in the common agreements that bind us together in community, the contingent verisimilitudes of rhetorical self-consciousness. These two sources of understanding are united by the fact that knowledge, whether it is of the higher mysteries of life or the mundane techniques of persuasion, is a form of power. Neither can be taken at face value. The unexamined idea is not worth holding.

If the sophists can be credited with discovering the individual, then Socrates must be credited with discovering the identification of virtue with wisdom, of morality with intelligence. At one level he appears to agree with the sophists in the belief that morality was more than mere social obedience. The destiny of the thinking being is to inquire after the grounds of action, to reach beyond the superstitions of tradition and mythology. The sophists err, according to Socrates, in opposing the good of the individual to that of the community. Rather, the two aspects of self, individual being and social character, are coordinates of the intelligent life. Virtue and wisdom can be identified because they spring from an even more basic identification, in the light of an active and inquiring intelligence, of communal and individual interests.

Unlike the Greeks, we think of virtue as a soft quality. To be good is to be harmless. As such, our notion of virtue is hemmed in by the legalisms of the age. It constrains rather than encourages behavior. The Greek concept *arete*, however, is vitally significant to life itself. It is not a passive state of being. It engages the self in all its manifestations, individual as well as social. As the basis of a civilization, *arete* inspires the conscious linking of thought to expression and the translation of both into action. It admits the existence of the passions. And it fosters the qualities of contemplation. So conceived, virtue is no mean thing. It is the essence of life itself.

This is no doctrine of self-sacrifice, of trading away personal desires in the interest of the common good. The Greeks understood that the generation of Athenians who flocked to the sophists did so because they were motivated by self-interest. They were hardened to exhortations by community leaders to do their part for their fellow citizens. Such appeals were as ineffective then as they are now. The vitally significant thing in a man's life is not the community but himself. And the solution to this new dimension of communal life is not simply to ban the sophists and the poets from some idealized state, as Plato does, or to force them to teach some brand of community ethic decided by a few moral authorities. The only way to replace a lifeless and irrelevant moral scheme is to find an ethic immune to the attacks of the most ruthless skeptic. The discovery of individual being among the debris of sophistication must daily prove a central fact of human behavior: the qualities of good citizenship—justice, wisdom, temperance, courage—are also the keys to individual advantage.

The primary moral conflict is not between the individual and the community. It is *within* the individual. The moral struggle takes place between the many partial selves, which the sophisticated mind activates as fragmentary impulses, and the coordinated self of intelligent, conscious purpose. The task is to bring within the precincts of the self-examining mind the notion that every individual is a society unto himself, every person is a crowd of conflicting emotions, ideas, desires, wants and aims. Moral responsibility is not responsibility to the social context of life. It is the responsibility of the individual to himself and, as such, transforms the burden of the mind coming to know itself. There is no virtue in living the life of fragmentary impulses, for it is always grounded in the past. It is a life of accommodation to unfulfilled, and unfulfilling, expectations. More important, such a life confines us to only a part of our selves, to regret, remorse and self-recrimination. In a sophisticated age, the moral life is that which completely fulfills one's present state of being. Integrity calls into service experience as well as heredity in order to be whole in one's character.

The process of coming to terms with sophistication begins with the examination of every aspect of life in community as if that inquiry matters for life itself. It is the only reasonable alternative for the attainment of self-knowledge. Moral responsibility is not a matter of free will. It relates means to ends, but in light of the individual's responsibility to himself. Life in a sophisticated age may be premised on change and utilitarian appearances, but we do not have to accept blindly and unquestioningly the power of contingent verisimilitude. We can be more than abdicators, subordinators or dominators.

The search for self is not a private matter, restricted to the single mind or the psychiatrist's office or even the like-minded support group. Its vitality as an instrument of self-knowledge, self-control and self-respect comes from its very public nature. Socrates roamed the streets and meeting places of Athens, seeking out anyone who would talk for awhile about the relationship between the higher ideals of philosophy and the mundane issues of everyday life. He believed and practiced that the unexamined life is not worth living, and that self-examination begins and ends in the context of politics as life in community. He was perhaps the most moral of men since his questions, pursued in earnest, stake his personal claim in their consequences. Within that framework, intelligence as an ethical ideal is a progressive norm. It ties individual development to the ever-increasing appreciation of the ultimate ideals that motivate each of us. We ought to be less concerned with defining and discovering the "good" than we are with finding and using the intelligent. After all, goodness tends to be a static state. Intelligence, however, moves the mind ever forward. It is the ability to adapt means to ends without becoming consumed by the techniques of adaptation or the temptations of intermediate aims.

The search for self can indeed become a selfish enterprise. In our sophistication we have frozen the dialectic between personal wants and the needs of community, even as we claim that enlightened self-interest is the basis for social progress. We pay lip service to enlightenment and proceed without pause to self-interest, self-assured that our actions are for the greater good. We are so caught up in the technologies of analysis and so fascinated by the instruments of change that we have lost sight of the predominant role ends must play in any community of independent, self-seeking minds—not simply the end of being virtuous since that would imply no change at all but, rather, the notion of "ending" itself. Lacking such a perspective, we have resurrected the social Darwinism of the late 19th century, adorned it in the vestments of 20th-century technology and produced the new rhetoric of contingent verisimilitude that supports our own success and explains the failures of others.

Successful living is often an exercise in the application of sophistic techniques that produce not self-knowledge but self-justification. "Who am I?" is no longer the question most people confront in the search for individual being. Rather, they are always asking "Who was I, in that specific instance, and what do others think of me?" Contemporary humanistic thought finds its cognate in the new science of chaos. Individual action is now random and often contradictory, controlled by the demands of immediate circumstances, the whims of transitory audiences and the logic of the contingent verisimilitude. The pattern of those random actions adds up in every case to a character unrecognizable to us. The sophisticated evasions built into politics and education and ethics prevent us from asking the question that has bothered thinkers since Socrates. Do we act out of knowledge of what is right or are we controlled by our concern for what others will think or say about us?

Sophistication need not cause despair for the self-seeking mind. The "knowledge of what is right" is neither good nor bad. It is simply a state of being defined at any moment by the flow of dialectical examination, of interaction between assertive individuals and passive communities. Intelligence is too often confused with resignation to disillusionment and the consciousness of impotence. We mistake cynicism for self-knowledge and by so doing dismiss ourselves from the task of understanding both the nature of our being as individuals as well as the dimensions of our character as social animals. But intelligence is an adaptive activity, a movement towards balanced self-expression and behavior. Ultimately, our happiness depends on the fact that "coming to know" is the highest form of consciousness. If intelligence is an ability to adapt means to ends, then happiness is success in the adaptation itself. It is intelligence on the move, not simply the knowledge of virtue or the contemplation of some perfect yet unachievable goal. Conversely, unhappiness comes not from the consciousness of sin but from the awareness of past stupidities. It is the psychological symptom of the failure to reach the real object of the good life. And what is the good life? You can only discover the answer, Socrates would remind us with characteristic irony, by following the advice of the oracle at Delphi. To know anything for certain, you must first know your self.

Selected Bibliography

In addition to the works of Aristotle, Plato, Thucydides and Plutarch available in several editions, the following books played a major role in the writing of this book:

Berlin, Isaiah. *The Crooked Timber of Humanity: Chapters in the History of Ideas.* Edited by Henry Hardy. New York: Alfred A. Knopf, 1991.

Boorstin, Daniel. *The Image: A Guide to Pseudo-Events in America.* 25th Anniversary Edition. New York: Atheneum, 1987.

Bowerstock, G. W. *Greek Sophists in the Roman Empire.* Oxford: Clarendon Press, 1969.

Brann, Eva T. H. *Paradoxes of Education in a Republic.* Chicago: University of Chicago Press, 1979.

Coby, Patrick. *Socrates and the Sophistic Enlightenment: A Commentary on Plato's Protagoras.* Lewisburg: Bucknell University Press, 1987.

Connor, W. Robert, editor. *Greek Orations.* Ann Arbor: University of Michigan Press, 1966.

Dewey, John. *Reconstruction in Philosophy.* New York: Henry Holt and Company, 1920.

_____. *Art as Experience.* New York: Minton, Balch and Company, 1934.

Durant, Will. *The Mansions of Philosophy: A Survey of Human Life and Destiny*. New York, Simon and Schuster, Inc., 1929.

_____. *Philosophy and the Social Problem*. New York: The MacMillan Company, 1917.

Ehrenfeld, David. *The Arrogance of Humanism*. Oxford: Oxford University Press, 1978.

Ewen, Stuart. *All Consuming Images: The Politics of Style in Contemporary Culture*. New York: Basic Books, 1988.

Farrar, Cynthia. *The Origins of Democratic Thinking: The Invention of Politics in Classical Athens*. Cambridge, England: Cambridge University Press, 1988.

Grant, Michael. *The Classical Greeks*. New York: Charles Scribner's Sons, 1989.

Guthrie, W. K. C. *Plato: The Man and His Dialogues, Earlier Period*. Cambridge University Press, 1975.

_____. *Socrates*. Cambridge University Press, 1971.

_____. *The Sophists*. Cambridge University Press, 1971.

Hubbard, B. A. F. and Karnofsky, E. S. *Plato's Protagoras: A Socratic Commentary*. London: Duckworth, 1982.

Iyer, Raghavan. *Parapolitics: Toward the City of Man*. Oxford: Oxford University Press, 1979.

Kagan, Donald. *The Outbreak of the Peloponnesian War*. Ithaca: Cornell University Press, 1969.

_____. *Pericles of Athens and the Birth of Democracy*. New York: The Free Press, 1991.

Kerferd, G. B. *The Sophistic Movement.* Cambridge University Press, 1984.

McKeon, Richard. *Rhetoric: Essays in Invention and Discovery.* Edited by Mark Backman. Woodbridge, CT: Ox Bow Press, 1987.

_____. *Thought, Action and Passion.* Chicago: University of Chicago Press, 1968.

Nill, Michael. *Morality and Self-Interest in Protagoras, Antiphon, and Democritus.* Leiden: E. J. Brill, 1985.

Philostratus. *Lives of the Sophists.* Translated by Wilmer Cave Wright. The Loeb Classical Library. Cambridge: Harvard University Press, 1921.

Powys, John Cooper. *The Meaning of Culture.* New York: W. W. Norton & Company, 1929.

_____. *A Philosophy of Solitude.* New York: Simon and Schuster, Inc., 1933.

Rankin, H. D. *Sophists, Socratics, and Cynics.* Totowa, New Jersey: Barnes & Noble Books, 1983.

Starr, Chester G. *Individual and Community: The Rise of the Polis, 800-500 B.C.* Oxford: Oxford University Press, 1986.

Stein, Leo. *The A-B-C of Aesthetics.* New York: Horace Liveright, 1927.

Voegelin, Eric. *The World of the Polis.* (Volume Two of Order and History). Louisiana State University Press, 1957.

_____. *Plato and Aristotle.* (Volume Three of Order and History). Louisiana State University Press, 1957.

White, Eric Charles. *Kaironomia: On the Will-to-Invent*. Ithaca: Cornell University Press, 1987.

Woodbridge, Frederick J. E. *Aristotle's Vision of Nature*. Edited by John Herman Randall, Jr. Westport, CT: Greenwood Press, 1983.

_____. *The Son of Apollo: Themes of Plato*. Woodbridge, CT: Ox Bow Press, 1989.